The Administration Of The English Borders During The Reign Of Elizabeth

Charles A. Coulomb

W0009704

Printing Statement:

Due to the very old age and scarcity of this book,
many of the pages may be hard to read due to the
blurring of the original text, possible missing pages,
missing text, dark backgrounds and other issues
beyond our control.

Because this is such an important and rare work, we
believe it is best to reproduce this book regardless of
its original condition.

Thank you for your understanding.

THE ADMINISTRÀTION OF THE ENGLISH BORDERS DURING THE REIGN OF ELIZABETH

A THESIS PRESENTED TO THE FACULTY OF THE GRADUATE
SCHOOL OF THE UNIVERSITY OF PENNSYLVANIA IN
PARTIAL FULFILMENT OF THE REQUIRE-
MENTS FOR THE DEGREE OF
DOCTOR OF PHILOSOPHY

BY

CHARLES A. COULOMB, Ph. D.

UNIVERSITY OF PENNSYLVANIA
D. APPLETON AND COMPANY, Agents, NEW YORK

1911

Copyright, 1911
By the University of Pennsylvania

J. F. TAPLEY CO.
NEW YORK

PREFACE

The history of the borders has heretofore been written with regard chiefly to the picturesque and romantic and with emphasis on those phases of it that tend to leave the reader with the impression that the north of England was an utterly wild and lawless region, the inhabitants of which, when they were not being raided by the Scotch, were taking revenge on their lowland neighbors.

Anarchy and disorder on the borders were, however, exceptional. It is intended, therefore, to give in this essay a brief account of the more orderly and usual administration of government by the properly constituted civil and military authorities, and to outline the various means by which the northern marches of England were protected, as well from domestic violence as from the raids and invasions by the Scotch.   C. A. C.

July, 1911.

CONTENTS

PAGE

Chapter   I.   The Geography of the Borders 1

Chapter   II. The Place of Ordinary Authority in the Administration of the Borders 16

Chapter III. The Office and Authority of the Wardens . 22

Chapter IV. Border Law 46

Chapter   V. Days of Truce 63

Chapter VI. Warden Courts 80

Chapter VII. The Defence of the Borders 91

Chapter VIII. Border Finance 110

Bibliography 120

Appendices 129

THE ADMINISTRATION OF THE ENGLISH BORDERS DURING THE REIGN OF ELIZABETH

CHAPTER I

THE GEOGRAPHY OF THE BORDERS

On November 18, 1558, Sir William Cecil, afterwards Lord Burghley, made a note of matters to be attended to on the entry of the queen to the crown. Very near the top of this list we find mentioned "The Borders of Scotland."

Being, as they were, the frontier of England toward Scotland, at that time a foreign country, the defence of the Borders for several hundred years formed an important part of the military policy of England; the most important of the nobility were called upon to administer their government; they absorbed in their administration and defence a considerable part of the revenues of the crown, and their population, reaching probably one hundred thousand at the time of Elizabeth, were subjected to an extraordinary military government in addition to the civil law of the realm. With the growing strength of government under the Tudors, and the changing relations with Scotland arising from the claim of Mary to the English throne, as well as the progress of the Reformation in Scotland, the administration of the Borders reached its highest development and its greatest importance. It is for this reason Cecil puts "The Borders of Scotland" among the first matters to be brought to the queen's attention.

In this memorandum Cecil probably uses the term with

the meaning it most often had, that is as a general name
for the northern part of England, including the counties
of Northumberland, Cumberland, and Westmorland, the
portions of Durham surrounded by Northumberland, and
the town of Berwick-upon-Tweed. At other times the
phrase was used as including the three marches and exclusive of Berwick; still again, it seems to have been used
with even less definite meaning.

For certain governmental purposes this part of England was divided into four military administrative districts. The first was the town of Berwick-upon-Tweed,
the chief military officer of which was its governor. Included under the jurisdiction of the governor of Berwick
were Holy and Farne Islands, outlying portions of Durham.[1] About fifteen miles south of the Tweed, Northumberland was divided into two unequal portions by an irregular line. This extended in a general east and west direction from the Scottish boundary just south of the Cheviot,[2]
to the mouth of the Alne River.[3] The portion of Northumberland to the north and east of this line was the East
March, while the Middle March included all the rest of
the county. Cumberland and Westmorland together
formed the yet more extensive West March. Of these
two counties Cumberland was of the greater importance
in Border affairs.[4]

The boundary line between the East and Middle
Marches was somewhat uncertain. In a memorandum on
the borders dated 1580, the boundary is given as coming
down by a small stream called Cawdgate, rising to the

---

[1] Calendar of Border Papers, Vol. II, No. 1429.
[2] The highest point of the Cheviot Hills, near their eastern end.
[3] C. B. P., I, 76.
[4] C. B. P., II, 1435. In this essay, "Borders" is used in a general sense, including the three northern counties and Berwick.
"Marches" is used when speaking of the specific divisions of the
three counties.

south of the Cheviot, thence to the River Till, thence to the north side of Bewick lordship, thence down the Warne to Warneford. The East borderers said, however, that the boundary went to Bewick and down the River Alne to Alnmouth, because of part of Alnwick lordship being mustered with the East March.[5] A commissioner appointed to investigate the administration of the Marches says, in 1550, "but of the perfect boundes betwene theis two marchies I coulde never be certeyne."[6]

The lists of towns and castles in the Marches which are from time to time found in the state papers seem to substantiate the claim of the East March to jurisdiction over the land between the Alne and the Warne.[7]

The phrase, "Debatable Lands," so often met with in dealing with affairs along the Borders, seems to have been used with various meanings. Almost at the end of the reign of Elizabeth, in 1597, we find it used to designate a portion of the land between the Esk and Sark Rivers at the extreme western end of the boundary line between the two Kingdoms, the ownership of which had been settled for nearly fifty years, and which continued to be called the Debatable Lands even in the reign of James.[8] This territory had, by a treaty made in 1552, been given to England as her share of a disputed peninsula between the two rivers just mentioned.[9] Each country got about four thousand acres,[10] "much of it as fertile as any in these North parts."[11]

There was, however, other ground along the borders

[5] State Papers, Borders, XX, 76.

[6] Report of Robert Bowes. Cott. Ms. Titus. F. 13, f. 160.

[7] Sadler State Papers, II, p. 19; State Papers, Borders, XX, 76; C. B. P., I, 162; C. B. P., II, 125.

[8] C. B. P., II, 598; C. S. P., Dom., Add., 1580-1625, Jas. I, XXXVII, 38.

[9] Rymer, Vol. VI, pt. iii, p. 223.

[10] C. B. P., II, 598.

[11] C. S. P., Dom., Add., 1547-1565, E. VI, II, 32.

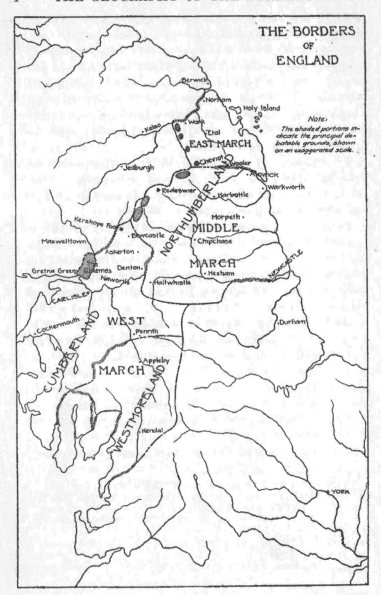

THE BORDERS
OF
ENGLAND

Note:
The shaded portions indicate the principal debatable grounds, shown on an exaggerated scale.

that continued through the reign of Elizabeth to be debatable in fact as well as in name. In the East March for example there seem to have been three well-known parcels, all situated near the point where the English-Scotch boundary leaves the Tweed and ascends the Reddenburn. One called the Midrigg contained about one hundred acres, a second, the Threape Rigg contained about three hundred acres, and a third, still further south, containing about one hundred acres.[12]

The Middle March also had three pieces of debatable ground along the Scotch boundary. Two lay close together near Cumberland, the third was near the boundary between the East and Middle Marches. In 1580, Sir John Forster said that he had sent Cecil a plot of the debatable ground in the Middle March.[13] There is also a statement that the Earls of Northumberland and Westmorland after their defeat in 1569, were driven to fly to the debatable lands between Liddesdale and England.[14]

There was also some debatable land in the West March. In 1592, we find a complaint from Lord Maxwell, a Scotch Warden, that some of the Graemes had wrongfully occupied three pieces of land,—one for thirty years of the value per annum of one hundred pounds Scots, another of twenty-five years standing of the value of two thousand five hundred pounds Scots, a sum equal to about six hundred twenty-five pounds sterling, and a third worth forty pounds sterling a year.[15]

These debatable lands were the source of much trouble for the wardens, since both the Scotch and English officers refused to listen to complaints brought by those of the opposite nation concerning spoilings in these pieces of territory. It was the business of each nation to keep

12 State Papers, Borders, XX, f. 138.
13 Ibid.
14 C. S. P., Dom., Add., 1566-1579, Eliz. XV, 117.
15 State Papers, Borders, XXVII, ff. 223, 224.

the subjects of the other from deriving benefits from the disputed land. Thus, Lord Grey in his orders to John Selby, Gentleman Porter of Berwick, in 1561, told him he was "to waste sufficiently the usurped ground."[16] In 1573, Sir Thomas Grey seized one thousand cattle which he claimed were feeding on English ground but which the Scots said were on Scots' ground.[17]

Sir William Bowes in a letter to Cecil, October, 1598, describes how some of this land came to be in dispute. He tells him that the Scotch made such raids that no Englishmen dare plant corn or pasture their cattle and that when the land is deserted by its former inhabitants "the Scots plant houses or keep their summer shieldings or stafherd their cattle or cut wood or hunt at their own pleasure."[18] In another case Robert Bowes said:—

"They [the Scotch] had sought also for right to damme theyr right course & channell of the water of Elterburne to make the same divert & alter his course into the ground of England to the ende to winne certyne ground called Water Haughes. Sr Rafe Ellerker vndammed the river & drave him to his old course."[19] Again, near Berwick, the Scotch moved certain of the boundary stones into English territory.[20]

In one or another of these ways, ground which was actually English might come into the nominal possession of Scotchmen and so become debatable. Sometimes an agreement was reached by which each nation pastured cattle on the ground in dispute, driving them home each night.[21]

[16] C. S. P., For., 1561-1562, 260.
[17] Ibid, 1572-1574, 1193.
[18] C. B. P., II, 1001.
[19] Sir Robert Bowes' Collection of Border Causes, No. 17, in State Papers, Borders, XX, 76.
[20] C. S. P., Foreign, 1566-1568, 1017.
[21] State Papers, Borders, XX, 76; Hamilton Papers, Scotch Record Publications, I, i, 54.

Many efforts were made during the reign of Elizabeth to divide the debatable lands. The first suggestion to mark the boundary was made in 1561, but nothing definite appears to have resulted from this attempt at settlement.[22] In 1564, a commission was granted to the Earl of Bedford and Sir John Forster to treat with Lord Maxwell and Mr. Justice Clerk for determining the boundaries between England and Scotland on the East and Middle Marches. Later, Randolph was added to the commission. Before anything was done, the negotiations of Elizabeth with the Protestant party in Scotland, following tne Scotch queen's marriage with Bothwell, and other more important international affairs interfered.[23] In 1575, we hear of another attempt at partition,[24] in 1580, of a third,[25] and again in 1597-98.[26] The union of the kingdoms under James seems to have occurred without the exact boundaries between them having been fixed.

The border counties, especially in the portions nearest Scotland, are rough and hilly. The deeper valleys run generally from southwest to northeast. Through the hills forming the steep sides of these valleys numerous streams have cut passes or gaps, extending for long distances at right angles to the principal valleys.

It was through these valleys and dales that the Scotch found their way into England, and it was to prevent such use of them that the English had constructed a line of more or less strong castles and towers which might be used either for defence against or refuge from the Scotch. Berwick was the most important of these de-

[22] C. S. P., For., 1561-1562, 260.
[23] C. S. P., For., 1564-1565, 381, 420, 549, 572, 665, 1040, etc.
[24] Ibid, 1575-1577, 554.
[25] State Papers, Borders, XX, f. 138.
[26] C. B. P., II, 1001; Rymer, VII, pt. i, p. 187. Letter of Queen Elizabeth to William Bowes.

fences. Situated on the north side of the Tweed within
the geographical limits of Scotland, the Berwick Bounds
included an irregular oblong of land containing about eight
square miles. The town of Berwick, situated at about
the middle of the base of the oblong, was a constant source
of care and expense to the queen, and a large part of her
expenditure in the North was chargeable to the construc-
tion and repair of its fortifications.

About six miles further up the Tweed is Norham Castle.
This was the strongest place of defence in the East March
and the various inspectors sent from London to view the
state of the borders, constantly call the attention of Lord
Burghley or Secretary Cecil to this fact and to the necessity of keeping the place in good repair.[27] Still farther
up the Tweed, near where it ceases to be the boundary-
line between England and Scotland, is Wark Castle. Of
the castles in the East March this was second only to
Norham in strength and importance. Concerning these
two castles, Robert Bowes reported in 1579 that "Norham
and Warke, the twoe principall and onlie places of strength
uppon this border are so greatlie in ruyns and decaid as
no man dare dwell in them, and yf spedie remedie bee
not had they will fall flatt to the ground." In the same
report Bowes estimates that it will cost twelve hundred
pounds to repair Norham.[28] Wooler, Newton, Pressen,
Dunham and Cornhill were depended upon by the warden
to aid in the supression of the thieves of Tevidale.[29] The
location of these castles and towers left a long stretch of
undefended territory between Harbottle Castle in the Middle March and Wark in the East March, so in 1580, it
was proposed that the queen should build three new towers
between Harbottle and the Tweed and one between Har-

27 C. B. P., I, 75. Cott. Ms. Calig. B. VIII, f. 384, dors.
28 Ibid, ff. 384, 395, dors.
29 C. B. P., I, 162.

bottle and the West March, the places available being small and the property of subjects.[30]

In the Middle March, Alnwick Castle was the residence of Lord Grey and Sir John Forster during their wardenships and was capable of caring for a considerable garrison, but it was nearly thirty miles from Scotland and hence ill-adapted to afford much protection to the English against raids of the Scotch.[31] This castle, now the chief residence of the Duke of Northumberland, is to-day one of the finest feudal fortresses in England, and the principal battery looks far over the valley of the Alne towards Scotland. Harbottle was much better situated, both as a castle against the Scot and as a menace to the unruly English of Tynedale and Redesdale. Sir Ralph Sadler in a survey made in May, 1559, urged its importance and suggested that it should have certain church lands of Durham annexed to it, in order better to provide for its keeper.[32]

Hexham was sometimes used as a military station but was too far from the border to be of much service.[33] Either Chipchase or Haltwhistle was commonly the residence of the Keeper of Tynedale, one of the deputy wardens of the Middle March. The Keeper of Redesdale, the other deputy, usually held Harbottle. Morpeth and Warkworth Castles were considerable places but are infrequently mentioned in the border papers of this period.

Carlisle Castle was the chief place of defence in the West March. The Wardenship of the West March and the Captaincy of the Castle of Carlisle were always in the hands of the same individual during the reign of Elizabeth.[34] In the West March was also the strong fortress

[30] State Papers, Borders, XX, 76.
[31] Cary's Memoirs, p. 96.
[32] Sadler State Papers, II, p. 15.
[33] C. S. P., For., 1558-1559, 1054.
[34] C. B. P., I, 785; State Papers, Borders, XX, 76.

of Bewcastle, situated in the northeast corner of Cumberland near the Scotch border.

This castle corresponded in situation to Wark in the East March. Naworth Castle and Lanercost Priory were farther south and were usually kept by one of the two warden-serjeants of the West March. Upon the treason and flight of Leonard Dacre in 1570, Naworth ceased to be inhabited, and in 1580 is described as being dilapidated. After the accession of James the castle was restored to Dacre's family in the person of Lord William Howard who had married a niece of Lord Thomas Dacre. Lord Howard restored the castle and continued to live there until his death in 1640.[35] The other warden-serjeant, the Land-serjeant of Gilsland, occupied Askerton Tower at Gilsland to protect the Cumberland farmers as much from domestic as from foreign violence.[36]

In a list found in the State Papers there is a total of about one hundred castles, and towers of less improtance, that were counted upon to aid in the defence of the borders. The abbeys and priories were almost always fortified, as their ruins indicate, and Scott speaks even of the great cathedral far to the south, as

"Time honored Durham
Half house of God, half castle 'gainst the Scot."

Included within the bounds of the three marches but administratively separate from the authority of the wardens were little islands of territory whose keepers, like the wardens, appear to have owed their appointment directly to the sovereign. Thus, Robert Bowes writes in 1580, "The L. Warden is by the wording of his patent

---

[35] "Household Books of Sir William Howard," Surtees Soc. Pub., Vol. LXVIII, pp. 365-393; C. S. P., Dom., Add., 1580-1625, Eliz. XXVII, 44; "House of Howard," pp. 543, et seq.
[36] C. B. P., I, 162; C. B. P., II, 982.

ordayned chefe Steward of all the princes Lordshippes, manors & landes wthin his precinct not otherwise disposed to any particular person.''[37] The result of their independence was in some cases serious interference with the government of the marches, both through the encouragement to evil-doers and through the less effective administration resulting from divided authority.

In the East March the most important of these franchises was Norham. Sometimes we find Norham and Holy and Farne Islands grouped together under the name of ''Norham and Islandshire.''[38]

These places, as John Cary explained to Burghley, formed a liberty within themselves, belonging to the Bishop of Durham, and ought to be in the hands of the Warden of the East March.[39] Besides its captain, Norham had a sheriff, escheator, coroner, steward and bailiff.[40] Justice was administered by the captain and his officials and even the governor of Berwick had no authority beyond the middle of the long bridge over the Tweed except with the consent of the captain of Norham.[41] Sir Henry Percy, who was captain in 1564, succeeded in maintaining his claim that Tweedmouth was part of Norham and out of the jurisdiction of the Governor and Council of Berwick.[42] Lord Hunsdon avoided this sort of trouble by having his son appointed to the captaincy of Norham.[43]

Hexham and Hexhamshire in the Middle March was independent until 1572, when it had its privileges taken away through annexation to Northumberland by the Act of 14 Elizabeth, Chapter 13, in which it is described

---

[37] State Papers, Borders, XX, 76.
[38] Sadler State Papers, II, p. 14.
[39] C. B. P., II, 34.
[40] Burghley Papers, Haynes, I, p. 397.
[41] C. B. P., I, 838; C. B. P., II, 31.
[42] C. S. P., For., 1564-1565, 196.
[43] C. B. P., II, 25.

as a County Palatine. It had just previously been ac-
quired by the crown through an exchange of lands with
the Archbishop of York.[44] The town of Hexham had been
granted by Henry VIII to Sir Reginald Carnabie, in 1538,
on the dissolution of the monastery.[45] It was too far from
the border to give much difficulty to the warden during
the few years of its independent position after the accession of Elizabeth.

In the West March we find three important districts
independent of the warden or nearly so. Bewcastle, the
most important of these, was situated just at the point
where the Scotch thieves of Liddesdale or the English of
Tynedale would be most apt to enter and rob or murder
the Cumberland farmer. The captaincy of Bewcastle had
been granted to Sir Simon Musgrave of Eden Hall before
Elizabeth came to the throne.[46] We find constant complaint from the warden to the Privy Council concerning
the sins of omission or commission on the part of one
who should have been his foremost supporter.

In June, 1584, for example, Lord Scrope, as warden,
prayed that Sir Simon might be called before the Council
to take orders that some sufficient person be despatched to
be in charge of Bewcastle for its better defence.[47] Thomas
Musgrave, son of Sir Simon, was, in 1593, commanded
by the Council to submit to Lord Scrope,[48] who appears
to have had no remedy in his own hands against Musgrave.
In another letter Lord Scrope requested Burghley to answer and give directions to Musgrave regarding the latter's
desire to take revenge on the Scotch for thieving.[49] Not

[44] Statutes of the Realm, Vol. IV, pt. ii, p. 604; C. S. P., Dom.,
Add., 1566-1579, Eliz. XXI, 44.
[45] "The Priory of Hexham," Surtees Soc. Pub., Vol. 44, pt. i, App.
p. CLXV.
[46] C. B. P., I, 434.
[47] Ibid, 225.
[48] Ibid, 935.
[49] Ibid, 968.

long after, in 1595, the Privy Council wrote to Scrope stating that Musgrave was accused of conniving at Scotch raids into England and requesting him to suggest some one to take his place.[50]

Almost as much difficulty came to Lord Scrope over Gilsland Barony. There was some dispute as to the official relationship of the land-serjeant of Gilsland to the Warden. We find a statement that the land-serjeant was an officer of the warden in Lord Dacre's time, and the counter-statement that the warden never had anything to do with Gilsland.[51] Whatever may be the truth of the matter, Lord Scrope treated the land-serjeant, Thomas Carleton, with a great deal of consideration, consulting with him as to the measures of defense and protesting to the Privy Council about Carleton's lack of respect for him instead of taking more summary measures.[52] Gilsland included much territory near the Border. Fourteen or fifteen manors and their bailiffs and a great number of tenants were under the land-serjeant's jurisdiction as Marshal Steward.[53] Among other duties, he was to have the martial government of all the queen's tenants, he was to reside within the barony and was to prosecute all murders by Scots to the boundary; if by others he was to seize them and deliver them for trial,[54] a power almost as extensive as that granted to the warden himself.

A broken clan,[55] known as the Graemes or Grahams, had dwelt in the land between the Esk and Sark for years and had maintained their independence against both the English and Scotch wardens. After the division of the territory those dwelling within the English portion refused

[50] C. B. P., II, 110.
[51] Ibid, 825.
[52] C. S. P., For., 1572-1574, 366, 1563.
[53] C. B. P., II, 824.
[54] Ibid, 982.
[55] A broken clan was one without any acknowledged chief.

to answer to the warden, claiming to be the queen's tenants and holding authority from her just as immediately as the warden did.

Thus we read that in 1562 the chiefs refused to answer for their surnames or for their whole clan but would only be responsible for themselves, their sons, or their servants.[56] Again about twenty years later there is evidence of the same independence. Lord Herries, the Scotch warden, wished to make an arrangement with the Graemes to behave themselves while he was in pursuit of certain Scotch rebels and they agreed with Lord Scrope to wait twenty days till he could communicate with London before they replied to Lord Herries' offer.[57] Affairs seem to have grown worse instead of better with the lapse of time, for in May, 1601, all the most important gentlemen in Scrope's wardenry joined in a petition to the Privy Council in which, among other things, they said that the Graemes contemned the government and warrants of the Lord Warden and ill-treated his ministers. ''They take upon them law dayes and undeasent orders emongst themselves and never will appeare either at assize or sessions.''[58]

For some reason, Elizabeth treated the Graemes with great consideration in spite of the trouble they were continually giving her wardens.[59] The state papers contain many complaints similar to the above. James I, who had little or no cause to worry about the borders or their defence, removed most of the Graemes to Ireland in 1607-1608.[60]

[56] C. S. P., For., 1561-1562, 995.
[57] C. B. P., I, 221.
[58] C. B. P., II, 1372.
[59] Acts of the Privy Council, 1597, p. 344; C. B. P., I, 845; C. B. P., II, 424.
[60] For an account of the transportation of the Graemes to Ireland, see "The Condition of the Borders at the Union, and the Destruction of the Graham Clan," by John Graham, London, 1907.

That there were many other franchises of less importance in the North appears by references in the records to leet courts, private escheats, and other similar evidences of the possession of the inferior regalities.

CHAPTER II

Before considering the question of the martial government of the Borders we wish to speak of the civil and crim-
inal jurisdiction exercised in that part of England by the
usual royal and county officers.   It is to be kept in mind that
the division of the counties of Northumberland, Cumberland and Westmorland into marches was for special military purposes resulting from their peculiar geographical
position on the boundary between England and what was
then a foreign country.

In all cases in which the safety of the kingdom was not
concerned, either through treason from within or invasion from without, the county orginazation retained at
least its nominal authority, and enforced the common and
statute law of the realm to the best of its moderate ability.

The usual legal processes went on in the Borders as
elsewhere in England, while the extraordinary authority
of the warden and his officers rested on this county organization like a net work, often entangling everyone
concerned in the meshes of conflicting jurisdictions.   In
a note on the Borders made about 1580, we find, for example, the following statement: "The manner of execution of the Lawes and administration of justice in the
Borders is all wth yt in thother Cowntyes of the Realme.
The Justices of peace Sheriffes of Shires Eschetes Coroners etc. and all officers of Corporations exercise theyr
authoritie according to theyr jurisdiction.   And the Assizes are yearelie kept as in other places."[1]

[1] State Papers, Borders, Vol. XX, 76.

In the first place, there is evidence that quarter sessions
and courts of oyer and terminer and gaol delivery were
held with considerable regularity.[2] For example, in 1559,
Lord Eure requested that a commission of oyer and terminer might be addressed to him and to others for the
administration of justice, "as well by the laws of this realm
and the statutes of the town of Berwick as by martial
law," and the Earl of Bedford makes a like request in
1564.[3] On the last four days of July, 1561, the President
of the North and his Council kept a quarter sessions at Alnwick in the Middle March, where twenty-four offenders
were condemned of whom certain ones were removed to Durham,[4] and, presumably, the others were executed. The
Sheriff of Northumberland could hold his county court
either in Newcastle, Morpeth, Alnwick or Hexham.[5] Fines
and amercements of sessions and gaol deliveries were
given to the sheriff as part of his allowance. We also read
of an assize being held at Carlisle, in 1584, in which Simon
Graeme and others were convicted before Mr. Justice
Clenche, and Mr. Francis Rodes, Sergeant at Law, the
queen's justices, of murdering George Graeme, and in 1591,
we find that "Simon Grame alias Symme of Medhoppe,
John Grame alias Jock of Medhoppe," and others were
indicted for having committed "sondry murders and
ffellonyes."[6]

By 1590, the practice of holding sessions at Alnwick
had apparently been discontinued. In June of that year,
Sir John Forster captured a "coyner" and two murderers.
He detained the counterfeiter until he received instructions
from the Privy Council, and sent the murderers to Dur-

[2] C. S. P., For., 1564-1565, 320; ibid, 1572-1574, 603, 1232, etc.
[3] Ibid, 1558-1559, 204.
[4] Ibid, 1561-1562, 367.
[5] Ibid, 1562, 1393.
[6] C. B. P., I, 252, 256, 352; State Papers, Borders, XXVII, f. 50.

ham for trial.[7] In 1596, Lord Eure, who had succeeded
Forster as warden of the Middle March, sent Lionel Carleton to Durham to be tried for burglary, and later re-
quests that gaol deliveries be held at Hexham or at Newcastle.[8] This request was probably granted, for, in July,
1602, John Cary spent three days at the Newcastle assizes.[9]
In the West March the assizes continued to be held at
Carlisle. In July, 1597, two thieves escaped from jail
during the assize in that city and in 1600 we read that
one Wattie was held for trial at the Carlisle assizes for
stealing a horse.[10]

The ordinary administration appears to have retained
its jurisdiction even over affairs in which the military
officers themselves were concerned. In 1597, a military
officer, Sir William Selby, Gentleman Porter of Berwick,
was bound to answer at the next assizes for raising a disturbance during the meeting of the English and Scotch
Commissioners at Berwick.[11]

The justices at times must have been impatient of
the martial authority of the wardens if we believe the
complaint of Richard Lowther, acting warden of the West
March in 1592. In a letter he asks Burghley to write
to the justices of assize to show him countenance for the
better advancement of her majesty's service, without which
he would be unable to perform the expected good offices.[12]

On the other hand the civil administration often called
upon the military one for aid. Sometimes the sheriff
and warden together could not secure the appearance of
offenders.[13]

7 C. B. P., I, 73.
8 C. B. P., II, 203, 617.
9 Ibid, 1477.
10 Ibid, 682, 1241.
11 Ibid, 498, 499, 500, 513, etc.
12 C. B. P., I, 749.
13 C. B. P., II, 1241, 1386.

The assizes in the north were held but once a year,[14] and the right of hearing appeals was reserved to the Privy Council.[15] Other references to the ordinary judicial processes are frequent.[16]

We find also that there is the usual complement of county officials. In 1562, a bill was proposed touching the Sheriffs of the North which aimed at fixing more definitely their powers. This does not appear to have passed into an act.[17]

In 1603 Sir William Selby, who had a dwelling and residence in Kent, was appointed Sheriff of Northumberland. He was relieved of that part of his oath requiring residence in Northumberland and could appoint a deputy-sheriff or sheriffs.[18] The sheriffs of all the northern counties were required to accept search warants for persons wanted by a warden and to bring them to the latter's residence.[19] There is besides constant reference in the state papers to the sheriffs in the north.[20]

The bailiffs of the queen's manors were to account for escheats to the queen, but they must have been derelict in their duties, for both in the East and in the Middle March there were complaints that the wardens or their officers converted escheats and seizures to their own use instead of accounting for them to the queen.[21]

The coroner was another official who had his usual duties to perform in the marches. In 1584, the queen's coroners in Carlisle found that George Graeme came to his

[14] Ibid, 862.
[15] C. S. P., Dom., Add., 1580-1625, Elizabeth XXX, 106.
[16] C. S. P., For., 1564-1565, 320; ibid, 1572-1574, 603, 1232; C. B. P., I, 240; C. B. P., II, 1267, etc.
[17] C. S. P., For., 1562, 1393.
[18] Egerton Papers, Camden Soc. Pub., XII, 389.
[19] C. S. P., Dom., Add., 1580-1625, Eliz. XXXII, 59.
[20] C. B. P., I, 643, 721; C. B. P., II, 523, 1386, etc.
[21] Ibid, 746, 1267, 881.

death by being struck between the shoulders by Richard
Graeme with a spear worth twenty pence and so felled
to the ground, and when he tried to arise Simon Graeme
struck him in the calf of the left leg with a sword worth
seven shillings and four pence.[22] In a letter dated the
same year we read that coroner's inquests had long been
held in Berwick.[23]

In 1597, in a memorandum proposing reforms on the Borders, it is stated that "it is fytt th't a clarke of the M'
Kette be erected for there is no sutch officer in Northumb."[24]   This was done so that a market court might be
held.

In spite of all this evidence that the ordinary forms
of government existed in the marches, there is an abun-
dance of other evidence that its actual administration was
neither energetic nor successful.   There was, for example,
the difficulty that the gentlemen of the marches were
ignorant of legal procedure.   Thus, in 1596, Lord Eure,
in a letter to the Privy Council, said that there was
no justice of the peace able to give a charge at a session
or to aid the gentlemen on any point of law.   He returned the Commission of the Peace that had been sent
to Sir John Forster, and requested a new one to include
himself and George Lightfoote, "a lawyere of whome we
stand greate need, whoe lyeth in Busshopricke, and none
nearer hand."[25]   On another occasion it was urged that
the Justices of the Peace should attend sessions quarterly,
under bond, and otherwise perform their duties.[26]

[22] C. B. P., I, 232.
[23] Ibid, 230.
[24] State Papers, Borders, XXXV, f. 157. The value of a personal
chattel that caused the death of any person was assessed by the
jury and was to be forfeited to the Crown. Originally the money
was devoted to religious or charitable purposes, whence arose the
name *deodand*, i. e., *Deo dandum*, to be given to God.
[25] C. B. P., II, 194.
[26] State Papers, Borders, XXXV, f. 157.

A more serious trouble was due to the venality of the justices. An anonymous letter to the queen, dated 1597, complained that the justices "keep no order for quarter sessions"; that they remove no forcible entries; that they take no care of markets nor reform the rates of corn; and that they release unbailable felons on insufficient bonds, of which the queen gets not one groat. In evidence of this the complainant said that the queen's itinerant justices will tell her that a Northumberland bail is as good as a queen's pardon.[27] In this same letter we find evidence of what appears to be a rather general survival of the leet or manorial court. The writer finishes by saying that every warden officer and "every larde that hathe but a leet court" is absolute lord of all escheats and the queen gets the least.[28] No other mention of leet courts was found, although the private bonding of thieves by certain lords, of which much complaint was made by the wardens, may imply the existence of such courts.

[27] C. B. P., II, 881.
[28] Ibid.

CHAPTER III

Besides the usual form of government, the peculiar location of the marches and the circumstances under which the northern counties had been made definitely a part of the nation of England had brought about the organization of a special form of semi-military administration.[1]

The chief officer of this organization was called the Warden. The number of wardens at any one time had varied during the history of the office from one to three. Early in the reign of Elizabeth, however, the council finally settled on the policy of appointing a warden for each of the three marches and of making them independent of each other within their several marches. During the reigns of Elizabeth's predecessors it had been the custom to appoint these officials from the head of the great border families, such as the Percies, the Dacres and the Nevilles. At her accession the West March had Lord Dacre for its warden, while the Wardenships of the East and Middle Marches were combined under Thomas Percy, Earl of Northumberland. There was some suspicion of the loyalty of these officers to the new queen and her policies, and there is evidence that this distrust was on account of the religious sympathies of the wardens.[2] The next year Cecil wrote to Sir Ralph Sadler, who was on a tour of investigation in the North, that the Warden of the East March would be permitted to come to London after he had ended his commission and that he (Cecil) would gladly

[1] In this connection it is interesting to note that these counties were divided into wards instead of hundreds or wapentakes.

[2] Sadler State Papers, I, pp. 410, 449, 452; C. S. P., For., 1558-1559, 1346, 1351.

have something against the Warden of the West March
at his (Sadler's) coming up.[3]

In a report dated a few days later Sadler suggested
new incumbents for the East, Middle and West Marches,
all of them from the northern counties.[4] Evidently the
new policy had not yet been formulated, for we find that,
following these recommendations, Sir John Forster of Bam-
borough was made Warden of the Middle March and had
the Keeperships of Tynedale and Redesdale annexed to
his office,[5] and Lord Grey of Wilton was appointed to the
Wardenship of the East March. No change was made in
the West March.[6] In 1563, Valentine Brown was sent
to survey the state of the Borders. In a report to Cecil
he recommended that the wardens should be southern men
for the reason that there would be less danger from the
disaffected nobles and others and that there would be
better order, for the southern men could do better with
one thousand men than the border lords with fifteen hundred.[7] The selection of wardens from other than border
counties now became the policy of Elizabeth, for while
Sir John Forster was not finally removed from office until
his increasing incapacity compelled that step to be taken
in 1595, no further new appointments as wardens were
made from the border nobility.[8]

The wardens appear to have been selected by a vote
of the Privy Council, as is indicated in a letter of Sir
Robert Cary to Cecil in which the former asked the Secretary to vote for him for the office of Warden.[9] There

---

[3] Sadler State Papers, I, p. 460.
[4] C. S. P., For., 1558-1559, 1409.
[5] C. B. P., II, 122.
[6] C. S. P., For., 1561-1562, 260.
[7] Ibid, 1563, 887.
[8] A list of the wardens of each march during the reign of Elizabeth is given in Appendix A.
[9] C. S. P., Dom., Add., 1580-1625, Eliz. XXXIII, 19.

seems to be no doubt, however, that Elizabeth's personal wish was often the deciding factor. Lord Hunsdon died in 1596, after being Warden of the East March for thirty years and Robert Cary, who had been commissioned as deputy warden, was very anxious to get his father's place. His importunities resulted in Elizabeth's sending him the following characteristic letter :—

"We doo wish you once againe to leave this course of peremptorie writings and doo command you to doo as you ought, for we that can judge what is fitt for you, will doo thinges as we please and when we please. Let these things therefore be perfourmed by you which you shall find by the treatie you ought to doo, and without any further importunitie and as William Bowes and Robert Bowes shall at any time direct you. And that being ended you shall then knowe what shall become of you."[10] Not long afterwards Lord Willoughby was appointed to the place that Cary had sought.

Once having been commissioned, the warden could not resign his office when he felt so disposed,[11] nor did even the notice of his supersession relieve him of his duties until the arrival of the new warden.[12]

The Governorship of Berwick was usually in the hands of the Warden of the East March and the Captaincy of the Castle of Carlisle in that of the Warden of the West March. The two latter offices were not held separately after the accession of Elizabeth, nor were the two former except when *ad interim* appointments of a deputy governor and a deputy warden were made.[13] Sometimes, however, the commission as Governor of Berwick was not granted

---

[10] C. B. P., II, 651.

[11] Letter of Hunsdon to Burghley; Ellis' Original Letters, Series II, Vol. III, No. 221, p. 105.

[12] Burghley Papers, Haynes, I, p. 2; C. B. P., II, 145, 154.

[13] C. B. P., I, 785; Burghley Papers, Haynes, I, pp. 374, 375.

till some time after the commission as warden or *vice versa*.[14]

The powers of the warden were defined in his commission of wardenry; in the instructions sent him from time to time by the queen or Privy Council; in the statutes applicable to the marches; in various treaties made with Scotland referring to border affairs; and, finally, in certain customary powers which the wardens from time immemorial had exercised.

The commission was a long and wordy document and when it was issued generally included any powers or special methods of procedure which up to that time had been settled by treaty with Scotland. Excepting such difference, the commissions are much alike in text.

In the commission granted to Lord Hunsdon to be Warden of the Middle March during the trial of Sir John Forster, in 1587, he was given all the power and special commandment to do and to execute all that was usually done by the warden and keeper in the reigns of Richard II, Henry IV, Henry V, Henry VI, Edward IV, Richard III, Henry VII, Henry VIII, Edward VI, and Mary; to correct, reform or amend by the seizure of lands, goods or chattels; to listen to all pleas, plaints or debates; in case of imprisonment or other hostile acts to hear and determine the same; to hold warden courts and sessions in whatsoever place he saw fit (in the Middle March), to inquire concerning offences against the truce made between England and Scotland; and to correct by punishment of persons or distress of goods for the preservation of the truce and the safety of the borders; he was empowered to levy all sums incurred by breach of ordinances by officers, and to chastise and punish those who refuse to obey and to certify them to the queen and Privy

14 Cary's Memoirs, p. 88; "Services and Charges of Lord Grey of Wilton," Camden Soc. Pub., Vol. 40, Appendix, p. 53.

Council if they still refuse obedience; and to search out
and punish traitors; he was to determine all pleas, plaints
and debates according to the custom of the marches; was
to set and appoint watchmen to give notice of raids from
the enemies and others, to explore and give notice of raids
at the cost of her liege subjects (in those parts). For
the safety of Berwick and Carlisle, when these castles
shall be threatened or attacked, all fencible men between
the ages of sixteen and sixty in the said marches were
to be mustered, and all men at arms, armed bill-men and
archers every of them according to state, degree or condition to be armed with competent armor, to be marshalled
in thousands, hundreds, and twenties, to be kept so as
to be ready to march for the defence of Carlisle or Berwick.
Those so marshalled could be compelled to serve by imprisonment or by other ways and means. The warden was
empowered to agree upon truces from week to week, two
weeks to two weeks, three weeks to three weeks, or from
month and months to month and months; to better enable
him to carry out the duties of his office he was to appoint
two deputies or substitutes and two warden-serjeants and
also all other officers necessary and expedient to perform
duties that have been accustomed to be done; and he was
to hold office at the pleasure of the crown. For perform-
ing all these duties he was to receive five hundred marks
per annum, ten pounds yearly apiece for his two deputies,
and forty shillings apiece yearly for the two warden-serjeants, to be paid semi-annually. In closing, all are commanded to give Lord Hunsdon obedience.[15]

Besides this rather extensive commission it was often
and perhaps always supplemented by special instructions.
For example, Lord Grey was told in 1560, in addition to
other things, that he was to obey the authority of the
Lieutenant General, the Duke of Norfolk, who in all mar-

[15] Rymer, Vol. VII, pt. i, p. 6.

tial cases was to use the advice of the Lord Warden and
that he was also to show favor and encouragement to all
borderers who are disposed to take the part of Scotland
against the French and the reverse to all who neglect it.[16]
A set of instructions, issued in 1597, indicates that the provisions of the warden's commission or of the treaties
had been neglected. These admonitory instructions provided that monthly days of truce should be held; that the
warden could issue letters of reprisal in case of default
of the Scotch warden; that the warden was to prosecute
English thieves in Scotland and to agree with the Scotch
warden to punish Scots harboring English march traitors;
at each day of truce redress was to be demanded against
murderers, burners of houses, perjurers, and those "thrice
fyled" (or foul).[17] The warden was to do his best to
fyle[18] on honor, the Scotch warden doing the like; to make
no delivery except on days of truce on receiving the like;
to seize the goods and flocks of Scotsmen stafherded within
the marches and forfeited by the treaties; to punish receivers of Scotsmen or those who have Scotch servants;
to keep a warden court half yearly or oftener if need be;
to account yearly to the auditor and receiver at Newcastle
of escheats for march treason. Challenge was not to be
denied to anyone accused of march treason nor were any
such to be released without the queen's pardon or warrant;
if any should escape, his jailer and warden-serjeant were
to be responsible; and, finally, the warden was to be
anually sworn to perform these duties at open assizes,
and four fit gentlemen of the wardenry were to be joined
in council with the warden.[19] Sometimes secret instruc-

[16] Cott. Ms., Calig. C. III, f. 107, et seq.; Calig. C. I, f. 153;
Burghley Papers, Haynes, I, p. 229; C. S. P., For., 1559-1560,
p. 359n.
[17] In all these cases the punishment was death.
[18] "To fyle" a bill was to declare guilty the person accused in it
of having committed some offence.
[19] C. B. P., II, 746; State Papers, Borders, XXXV, f. 157.

tions were given to the wardens to take revenge in Scotland for raids which were unpunished by the Scotch wardens.[20]

The wardens were expected to reside within their marches during the term of their commission unless the queen gave special permission for them to be absent. This permission seems to have been granted very reluctantly and only for good cause. Lord Scrope, for example, on being appointed Warden of the West March in 1563, found the Castle of Carlisle in very bad order. He was therefore permitted to go to his home at Bolton for twenty or twenty-one days until he might make proper repairs at Carlisle.[21] The next year the queen wrote to the Marshal of Berwick that the Earl of Bedford, Warden of the East March, might be allowed to go to Yorkshire for three weeks only.[22]

A few years later, Sir John Forster requested permission to leave his march, but Elizabeth demanded to know the state of the borders before permission would be granted.[23] Lord Hunsdon, in August, 1581, desired to be relieved of his wardenship owing to age and the necessity of staying at Berwick.[24] On another occasion, having come to London, he delayed his departure for his charge too long for Elizabeth's patience. Robert Cary writing to his father an account of his interview with her, said that "she grew yntoo a grete rage, begynnynge with 'God's wonds, that she wolde sett you by the feete, and send another yn your place if you dalyed with hyr thus for she wolde not be thus dalyed withall.' Robert tried to pacify her with explanations but, he said, she anseryed me 'that you have byn goynge from Crystmas to Ester, and from

20 C. B. P., I, 245.
21 C. S. P., For., 1563, 931.
22 Ibid, 1564-1565, 418.
23 C. S. P., For., 1566-1568, 1879.
24 C. B. P., I, 102.

Ester to Whytsontyd, but yf you dyfferde the tyme any longer, she wolde appoynt sume uther yn your place.' '' [25]

Even a writ commanding a peer to come to Westminster to attend Parliament did not justify him, if he was a warden, in leaving his post without special permission from the queen.[26]

The wardens had power to appoint certain of their subordinate officers. In the East March, in 1596, the warden could appoint his deputy warden [27] and the Marshal of Berwick.[28] At the beginning of Elizabeth's reign, however, the queen held the appointment of the deputy warden of the East March in her own hand and it does not appear that the warden himself was consulted.[29] The warden of the Middle March had a similar power, for both Sir Ralph Sadler and John Cary appointed their deputies on taking office.[30] Lord Hunsdon, however, in 1587, when he was temporarily warden of the Middle March, wrote twice asking the queen's permission to remove the deputy warden.[31] The naming of the Keeper of Harbottle Castle was a privilege also annexed to the Wardenship of the Middle March.[32]

In the West March, the deputy warden was usually appointed by the warden,[33] but if the queen objected to the person appointed, as she sometimes did, the warden hastened to appoint the man the queen preferred.[34] On one occasion Lord Scrope instead of appointing a deputy,

[25] Ellis' Original Letters, Series II, Vol. III, No. 220, p. 102.
[26] C. B. P., I, 263.
[27] C. B. P., II, 314; C. B. P., I, 537.
[28] Cary's Memoirs, p. 57.
[29] Sadler State Papers, I, pp. 708, 709; C. S. P., For., 1559-1560, 160, 161.
[30] Cary's Memoirs, p. 96; C. S. P., For., 1559-1560, 349.
[31] C. B. P., I, 574.
[32] Ibid, 398.
[33] Ibid, 743; C. S. P., Dom., Add., 1580-1625, Eliz. XXXII, 88.
[34] C. B. P., II, 760, 775, 787.

appointed a group of four gentlemen of Cumberland to have charge of the West March during his absence. After serving a few weeks, these four were to appoint another group of four, and so on, until the queen should decide whom she wished Lord Scrope to appoint as his deputy.[35] In spite of the definiteness of some statements in the evidence, one may say that the appointments were not made at the discretion of the warden, but were suggested to the court in the form of a nomination or request, which usually was approved.

The duties which took most of the time and attention of the wardens were the holding of the warden courts, which as we have just seen were the chief means by which they enforced their authority within the march; the holding of days of truce with the opposite wardens of Scotland; and the making and maintaining of proper provisions for the defence of their marches from raids or invasions from Scotland. These topics will be more fully treated in the following chapters.

In addition to these, it is possible to gather a long list of the other duties of the wardens covering all sorts of affairs, not only those connected primarily with their duties as military officers on the frontier, but also some which appear to have devolved on them as prominent persons of the realm that happened to be in a place where some piece of official work needed to be done.

Among the warden's military duties was that of taking charge of the mustering of the "fencible" men spoken of in his commission. These musters were intended to be held several times each year. The warden with the gentlemen of his march viewed the bands and their armor, carefully noting any deficiencies in either number or equipment, and sending complete reports to the Council.

Another duty of the same sort was the issuing of pass-

[35] Ibid, 1334.

ports or safe-conducts to Scotchmen to travel through England, either to London or on the way to the continent.
These were at one time issued at London.[36] For some
reason, however, possibly because of the trouble involved
in sending for them over such a long distance, their issuing
was turned over to the wardens. In the Statute 14 Elizabeth, Chapter 5, it was expressly stated that this right
was not to be interfered with.[37] The horses ridden by the
travelers are usually described with much greater particu-
larity than the travelers themselves,[38] probably owing to
the constant trouble over the sale of horses to Scotland as
indicated below.

The issuing of "plaquets" or permits for the sale of
English horses into Scotland was another of the warden's
duties. It was perhaps too freely exercised or else too
loosely controlled, for in the records are many complaints
about the practice, together with statements that the
Scotch would be unable to make raids without the English
horses and that three horses out of four on the Scotch
side were English.[39] This selling of horses into Scotland was considered so grave a danger that we find several
statutes passed with the object of preventing it.[40]

The warden also had power under his commission to
make reprisals on Scotland for unsatisfied claims of the inhabitants of his march and also to issue letters of reprisal
to despoiled tenants.[41]

The privilege of taking revenge was not an unused one,
as appears by many references to such raids by the wardens. Sometimes the provocation was great,—in one case
four hundred claims against Scotland were lying unre-

[36] C. S. P., For., 1558-1559, 701, 1293.
[37] Statutes of the Realm, IV, pt. i, p. 592.
[38] State Papers, Borders, XLI, f. 98; C. B. P., II, 1440.
[39] C. S. P., For., 1561-1562, 82, 85; C. S. P., II, 368.
[40] See below, p. 55.
[41] C. B. P., I, 192, 198, 234, 555; C. B. P., II, 298, 1423, etc.

dressed, and in another instance there had been no redress for injuries for fourteen years.[42]

On the other hand we find the warden using unnecessary cruelty in making reprisals. For example, when John Cary was serving as his father's deputy in the East March, in 1596, some horses were taken from within the bounds of Berwick and he could get neither the horses nor money for them. He took advantage of the musters held shortly after they had been stolen and made a raid into Scotland to the house of one of the four thieves and cut him in pieces.[43] Elizabeth much regretted this affair and told Cary that such revenge was "verie barbarous and seldom used emonge the Turckes."[44] On account of the international difficulties which invariably followed such reprisals, the wardens often found it desirable to get especial authority from the queen before making such attacks, and in one case Lord Scrope mentions as a secret that her majesty by Mr. Secretary had directed him, on any outrage being committed, to take such revenge as he could.[45] On another occasion Lord Scrope had made another raid into Scotland and had taken and hanged two Scotch thieves, upon which the King of Scots complained to the Privy Council. A little later, Lord Scrope wrote to Secretary Cecil concerning the King's complaint, "as yet we have but a leetle tickled him aboute the edges," and if they (the borderers) would not be quiet he did not mean to lie in their debt.[46]

In addition to these responsibilities connected more or less with their military positions, the wardens were charged with a number of less important duties. Sometimes they were called upon to prevent the escape into

42 Ibid, 520, 561; C. B. P., I, 745, 746.
43 C. B. P., II, 298; Cary's Memoirs, p. 76.
44 C. B. P., II, 329.
45 C. B. P., I, 156; C. B. P., II, 1191; C. B. P., I, 245.
46 C. B. P., II, 1423.

Scotland of malefactors or to search out those who had committed felony and to seize them and send them to the sheriff of the county in which the crime was committed or to the Council at London.[47]

In conjunction with the receiver of the queen's lands in Cumberland, Lord Scrope was directed, in 1597, to issue distress warrants for the rents of her majesty's tenants of Brough Barony,[48] probably under his commission as justice of the peace.

In another case Lord Grey, Warden of the East March, apparently sitting as a justice of the peace, ordered certain disputed lands to be divided, thereby settling an acrimonious quarrel between two of the gentlemen of the Middle March,—Sir Thomas Grey of Horton and Sir John Forster.[49]

The wardens also performed services on behalf of the Court of High Commission in hunting out recusants within their marches as well as serving on the Commission itself.[50] It must be confessed that their search became more effective after a few visits from the Bishop of Durham and the receipt of letters from the Privy Council. In 1585, for example, Lord Scrope could find only two recusants in the West March, which at that time probably contained at least thirty thousand inhabitants.[51] Ten years later, Lord Scrope sent to Toby Matthew, Bishop of Durham, the names and qualities of a multitude of obstinate recusants in Westmorland and Cumberland.[52] The good bishop was much worried over the difficulty of enforcing the law, and urged that "the writ *de excommunicato capiendo* and the

[47] C. B. P., I, 740, 442.
[48] C. B. P., II, 470.
[49] C. S. P., For., 1560-1561, 735.
[50] C. B. P., II, 1331; C. S. P., Dom., Add., 1580-1625, Eliz. XXVIII, 58.
[51] C. B. P., I, 313.
[52] C. B. P., II, 541.

execution followeing hereupon maie be caused to runne as
well in Northumb'land, Cumberland and Westm'land as in
the Bushoprick of Duresme & elsewhere and that not onlie
the Sheriffs but the wardens be commanded to see the same
executed."[53] The Statute does not appear to except the
northern counties from its operations, so perhaps the
trouble was due to the laxity of the sheriff in serving this
writ and in issuing executions upon it, since we find the
same sort of complaint against the sheriffs for not levying
on the property of those going on the bonds of prisoners.[54]

The enforcement of the laws against seminary priests
was also entrusted to the wardens.   Thus, in 1593, Cary
got hold of such a priest and asked Burghley's advice
about what to do with him, since he had no prison but
Haddock's Hole, a very bad place and only fit for thieves
and murderers.[55]

A certain authority in admiralty matters appears to
have devolved on the wardens, apparently by virtue of
their military office. For example, in 1559, a ship was
wrecked on the coast of Northumberland, and the Earl
of Northumberland, Lord President of the Council at
the North wrote to Ralph Sadler, acting warden of the
East March, instructing him to have the goods that remained viewed and valued and to punish those who had
stolen any of the cargo. Immediately afterwards, Lord
Clinton laid claim to the salved cargo which he claimed
belonged to him by virtue of his office of admiralty.[56]
A little later, the water-bailiff under Sir Ralph Grey,
at that time Warden of the East March, meddled with a
Scotch ship driven on shore in Bamburghshire near Ross,

53 State Papers, Borders, XXXIV, f. 228.
54 Cott Ms., Calig. D. I, f. 247.
55 C. B. P., I, 916.
56 C. S. P., For., 1559-1560, 197, 201, 202.

to which interference the Queen of Scots objects as well as the owners.[57] Again, in 1562, Lord Grey wrote to Cecil and stated that the men and townships involved had been assessed two hundred pounds to pay for their spoiling of a Scotch ship which had been wrecked near Berwick.[58] On another occasion Lord Hunsdon wrote to the Council acknowledging their order to stay all ships between York- shire and Berwick, whereof he was Vice-admiral, but that he had found none worth staying except at Newcastle, where he had stayed all ships and mariners. He also sent a list of their tonnage and crews and where the men dwelt.[59]

The water-bailiff just spoken of appears to have been the constable for admiralty cases, but was also used by the wardens as a messenger to carry letters or the rolls of cases to be tried at a day of truce to the Scotch warden. As such the bailiff had the right of free pas- sage through any Scotch or English march on his way to the warden's residence.[60]

In addition to the foregoing duties, the wardens claimed certain jurisdictions which led them into various disputes with other authorities. The conflict of authority arising from the existence within the marches of independent lordships, such as Bewcastle, Gilsland and Norham, has already been mentioned. Another dispute arose over the right of the warden to arrest an offender who had escaped from his own march. In several cases, the warden-ser- jeant arrested a man in Durham to answer at a day of truce;[61] in another instance, a man who had stolen goods in Scotland was arrested by the serjeant. After being

[57] Ibid, 1559-1560, 269.
[58] C. S. P., For., 1562, 288.
[59] State Papers, Borders, XXV, f. 188.
[60] C. B. P., I, 743.
[61] C. B. P., II, 1002.

released on bond, he stole in Berwick and was indicted for felony, but was delivered by the mayor of Berwick to the deputy warden to be turned over to the Scotch warden for punishment.[62] On the other hand it is stated that the Warden of the Middle March could not arrest those under the government of the East March, though it was admitted there were contrary precedents.[63] On one occasion the land-serjeant of Gilsland in the West March arrested a notorious thief in that march and delivered him to Lord Eure, Warden of the Middle March. This, though probably within the terms of the land-serjeant's patent, gave rise to much protest and correspondence with Burghley on the part of Lord Scrope, who finally convened a warden court, tried and executed two of the land-serjeant's friends and proclaimed as an outlaw Thomas Carleton, the land-serjeant himself.[64] Lord Scrope claimed that Lord Eure should have made a requisition on him for the arrest of the outlaw, a claim that is substantiated by articles of agreement entered into between the West and Middle Marches in 1571.[65]

It seems, therefore, that the martial law was superior to the civil law in cases where they came into conflict, but that the wardens were not to intrude upon each other's jurisdictions.

Still another difficulty arose from the appointment by the queen of general officers for military and other purposes in the north but who were not subject to the warden's authority. As an instance of this, we find, that, in 1596, Sir William Selby was appointed Comptroller of the office of Ordnance in the North. On sending his deputy to view the munitions at Carlisle, Lord Scrope would not permit the deputy to make his inspection and

[62] Ibid.
[63] Ibid, 231.
[64] Ibid, 452, 483, 529, 530, 533, 982, etc.
[65] Cott. Ms. Calig. C. III, f. 107.

protested that the deputy comptroller had intruded on the warden's office contrary to the express words of the latter's patent.[66] On another occasion Lord Hunsdon threatened to resign because Randolph, Elizabeth's ambassador in Scotland, had interfered with his authority.[67] Conflicts of authority between the warden as Captain of Berwick and the civil officers of the town also occurred from time to time. On one occasion for example the Captain complained to the mayor and freemen that they were compelled by their charter, among other things, to provide a prison and gallows for the use of the warden's prisoners, to keep all prisoners turned over to them by the Captain under a sufficient guard, to keep a pillory, to name six burgesses of the town within four days of Michaelmas to act as host for Scots permitted to come into the town by the Captain, and not to lodge Scotchmen without the permission of the Captain, all of which provisions he claimed to have been violated.[68] And in the years 1592 to 1595, we find a record of a series of quarrels between the warden and his officers and the corporation.[69]

Toward the end of the reign of Elizabeth, the final supremacy of the Protestant party in Scotland and the probable succession of James to the English throne seemed to bring about greater quietness on the marches. As a result of this progress toward law and order, the successive treaties made from time to time took more and more power away from the wardens. After the treaty of 1597, the last entered into between the kingdoms, we find constant complaints from the wardens that the justices of the peace are in charge of cases formerly within the jurisdiction of the wardens.[70] In the case of the mur-

[66] C. B. P., II, 358, 437, 439-445; cf. C. B. P., I, 764.
[67] C. S. P., For., 1572-1574, 423.
[68] Hist. Mss. Com. 12th Report, App. pt. IV, p. 52.
[69] C. B. P., II, passim.
[70] Ibid, 1101, 1152.

der of one Reveley, for example, Lord Willoughby, the
Warden of the East March, wrote to Cecil, saying that
the Northumberland justices challenged his dealings with
such cases and sent them to Newcastle to undergo the
law, and that there they found means of escape through
their friends and allies.[71]

Some dispute of this sort must have been the occasion
of a memorandum on the respective powers of the justices of the peace and the wardens which was made some-
time between 1590 and 1602.

Of the justices, this note says:—"The authoritie of a
Justice of Peace is directed by the Lawes of a Realme,
and lymited wthin the bounde of the Kingdoms.

"It is an ordinarie, civill but a slower kinde of Jur-
isdiccon.

"It enquires of Treasons but hath noe power to punish
them.

"It enquires of Fellonies, ryotts, routts, and vnlawfull
assemblies but noe punishment can be inflicted but in
open quarter Sessions wch are to be kept but fower tymes
in the yeare.

"It removes possessions violentlie and forciblie taken
for the time but still wth reference to the quarter Sessions.

"It restreynes men from fighting, and quarreling, by
pressing the parties (that have done, or are likelie to
doe anie of these disorders) to enter securities to kep the
peace; or in case they cannot fynde sufficient securitie
by committing them to prison, etc."

On the other hand the note states that "The authoritie
of the Warden is an extraordinarie Marshall and quick
power, grounded upon customs of the place, and consent

71 Ibid, 1250. The power of wardens to try cases involving life or
death was disputed as early as 1568,—C. S. P., For., 1566-1568, 2307,
2498.

of the Princes in sondrie Treaties for those causes, for defence of eyther Kingdom, from violence and force of the other. It cnteynes not it self wthin the bounde of the Kingdom, but reaches to the opposite frontire and pursues fellons wth freshe pursuite there alsoe.

" Either Warden hath euer vsed (and soe ought to doe) by a Kynde of correspondence, to send offenders wthin their seuerall Marches to the other, his opposite, upon demand, to be iusticed by him.

" There are Lawes wch they call Martch Lawes, such as haue beene agreed upon by Comissioners authorized from both Prynces. By these Martch or Martiall Lawes, the Warden maie upon the sodaine call a court, empannell a Iurie, by whom yf anie man offending wthin the wardenry, be found guiltie, yf it bee of fellonie or treason, he maie be forthwth executed by the Warden." [72]

The wardens were removable from office at the pleasure of the queen and there is not much doubt that the resignations that occurred from time to time were not only by the permission of the queen but also by her suggestion. As a rule, however, the appointments appear to have been for life or during the proper conduct of the warden in his office. Sir John Forster and Lord Hunsdon each held their wardenries for thirty years and the former was finally removed from office only after formal charges had been made against him on two occasions, and after he had been tried before a commission and found guilty of negligence in office.

The complaints on the first occasion, in 1586, cover a long list of offences in which Forster is charged with improperly holding days of truce, taking care of his own losses to the neglect of her majesty's tenants, and accepting too small penalties from the Scots, and he is also accused of securing the safety of his own goods by his

[72] State Papers, Borders, XLI, 1546.

leniency with the Scots. He is also charged with having sent corn, and other supplies over the border into Scotland and with permitting notorious Scotch thieves and murderers freely to resort to him.[73] As a result of these charges, his commission was suspended and Lord Hunsdon was appointed Warden of the Middle March. Forster was tried at Newcastle before a committee of the Council of the North.[74] He appears to have been cleared of the charges after his first trial and to have received back his wardenry. About ten years later there is another series of complaints from Forster's wardenry, charging him with a general disregard of the border law.[75]

He was ordered by the queen to put himself under the charge of her officers at Durham, practically placing him under arrest, and was shortly afterwards removed from his office and his place given to Lord Eure.[76]

The latter about a year later is himself charged with malfeasance in office and is impeached by jurors on four charges.[77] He asked for a trial before the queen and council,[78] but the matter was left to Sir William Bowes and the Bishop of Durham.[79] Edward Grey of Chillingham, one of the deputy wardens, was appointed acting warden, pending the settlement of the charges against Lord Eure. The latter appears to have resigned as a result of the charges against him, although there is no definite statement of his guilt.[80]

In addition to the interference with the duties of the

[73] State Papers, Borders, XXV, ff. 163, 164, etc.; Cott. Ms. Calig. C. IX, f. 315; C. B. P., I, 452, 453, 454, 455, 475, 493, 494, 534, 546, 494, etc.
[74] Ibid, 501.
[75] C. B. P., II, 211.
[76] Ibid, 197, 206.
[77] Ibid, 638, 652, 756.
[78] Ibid, 702, 762, 763, 764, 854.
[79] Ibid, 721.
[80] Ibid, 702, 772, 792, 854.

wardens arising from conflicts of authority within the marches, they were often subjected to interference in their offices by the Privy Council, and by the Council of the North.

The Privy Council interfered only spasmodically with the wardens and most of its interference appears to have taken the form of advice or suggestion. Early in 1559, for example, the Council wrote to the Earl of Northumberland, Warden of the East and Middle Marches, regretting the decay as reported in the muster roll and suggesting that he should get together a garrison in truth at Berwick.[81] The results of all musters in the marches were sent to the Privy Council, which considered them and usually inquired of the wardens the reasons for any default in the numbers of properly armed men.[82]

At other times, the Council sent notice to the wardens telling them how they should treat fugitives from Scotland,[83] or perhaps approving the request of a warden for the temporary loan of troops from Berwick or from one of the other marches.[84]

Sometimes, however, there was more direct interference with the warden. It is probable that in these cases the Council merely took cognizance of a complaint that had been addressed to Burghley or perhaps even to the queen. For instance, in 1583, the brother and wife of Arthur Graeme begged the Council for redress for his murder by Thomas Musgrave. Other complaints follow and finally the Council sent a letter to Lord Scrope, directing him to take action.[85] On another occasion the Council wrote

[81] A. P. C., 1558-1570, p. 39.
[82] Ibid, p. 16; C. S. P., For., 1575-1577, 128; C. B. P., I, 15, 26, 42, 43, etc.
[83] Ibid, 118, 267.
[84] A. P. C., 1558-1570, pp. 16, 23; C. S. P., For., 1558-1559, 104, 230; C. B. P., I, 152, 215, 486, 519, etc.
[85] Ibid, 157, 161.

to Lord Scrope, disapproving of his securing the repair
of castles and houses on the border by executing the penal
statutes, as that would be odious to the inhabitants. The
Council preferred to have the matter arranged by a commission.[86] Sometimes no redress for spoil or murder on
the marches was had for a long time. In one such case
the Privy Council directed the wardens to meet for the
redress of the most recent grievances, leaving those of
former years to be settled by a commission.[87]

The Council often interfered with what were apparently very trivial matters. The Privy Council in Star
Chamber, June 10, 1586, ordered Lord Scrope to settle a
dispute concerning some land between David Hinderson
of Malfarnes and Thomas Carleton.[88] A year or so later,
the Council ordered "a letter to Lord Scrope, Warden
of the Mydle Marshes praying his Lordship to examine
a cause betweene William Wyngfeild, an aged poore man,
and John Smithe for 2 acres of land, and to take suche
order that the said Wyngfeild maie be continued in the
quiett possession until he maie be evycted by due course
of lawe."[89] A few months afterwards the Council sent
another letter to Scrope ordering him to redress the stealing of some cattle.[90]

There is the possibility that this interference in the less
important matters was due to the fact that the wardens
constantly wrote to Lord Burghley or to Walsingham or
Cecil for advice, thus giving opportunity for such interference.[91]

[86] Ibid, 152.
[87] Ibid, 151, 272; A. P. C., 1597, p. 4.
[88] A. P. C., 1586-1587, p. 145.
[89] A. P. C., 1587-1588, p. 163.
[90] Ibid, p. 275. On one occasion the Council ordered Lord Eure to
secure the appearance of certain malefactors before them in Star
Chamber. A. P. C., 1595-1596, p. 98.
[91] C. S. P., For., 1572-1574, 292; C. B. P., I, 235, 673; C.
B. P., II, 1089, 1116, 1442, etc.

For example, in 1584, Lord Scrope took four Scotch thieves and in a letter to Walsingham, begs to have the disposal of them left to himself, which, he says, will be to good purpose.

On another occasion certain Rutherfords petitioned Sir Robert Cary to release a pledge, the bills for which he was held as surety having been satisfied. Cary thereupon wrote to the Council begging them not to interfere but to permit him to manage the affair himself.

According to a new order for the Council of the North adopted in 1560, it was to be composed of all the noblemen in the North. This is limited by the further statement that there is to be one from each Riding of York and one each from Durham, Cumberland, Westmorland and Northumberland. It was to have a President, Vice-President and two members learned in the law. The President or Vice-President and three others, of whom one of the men learned in the law was to be one, were to be of the *quorum*. The Council was to hold four sittings yearly, of which one was in Westmorland and Cumberland or else in Northumberland.[92] It was not necessary to have sessions both at Carlisle and Newcastle the same year.[93] The wardens were generally included in the Commission,[94] or were added to the Council after their appointment.[95]

The Council of the North had two duties in the marches. First, it sat as an assize court yearly at either Carlisle or at Newcastle and so can be considered as part of the ordinary government of the northern counties.[96] In ad-

[92] C. S. P., For., 1560-1561, 705.
[93] Ibid, 1561-1562, 145.
[94] A. P. C., 1558-1570, p. 27; C. S. P., For., 1560-1561, 905.
[95] C. B. P., I, 974.
[96] C. S. P., For., 1561-1562, 66. No attorney was to receive more than 16d. nor any counsellor more than 40d. in any one sitting for any one matter depending before the Lord President and Council. C. S. P., Dom., Add., 1566-1579, Eliz. XIV, 42.

dition to this it acted with something like the powers of
a grand jury over the martial administration of the Borders, inspecting and inquiring about the defences of the
marches and their decay and making reports thereof from
time to time to the queen and Privy Council.[97]

The President of the Council in the North was usually
also the Lord Lieutenant for the Northern Counties [98] and
as such the immediate military superior of the wardens,
who were in all things to obey him.[99] It was through
its president that the Council chiefly acted in border affairs either in making investigation as directed by Privy
Council, or in advising the latter from time to time of the
condition of the marches.[1] For example, in 1580, the
Earl of Huntingdon wrote to the Privy Council, stating
that the decay of horsemen on the Borders was most plain;
that nothing had been done by way of improvement, that
the difficulty was caused by leases by her majesty and
others to persons who look only to profit, breeding cattle
and not horses, and finally he recommended that a commission be appointed to divide the debatable ground and
to examine the laws of the Borders.[2] In other cases the
President of the Council called the wardens before him
to consider the evil administration of the marches and
to devise a remedy.[3]

Through his office as Lord Lieutenant, the President
of the Council of the North had still other authority over
the wardens,[4] which, however, does not appear to have
been exercised without special direction from the queen

[97] C. S. P., For., 1561-1562, 66; C. B. P., II, 97.
[98] C. S. P., For., 1560-1561, 905; C. B. P., I, 565; C. B. P.,
II, 163.
[99] Burghley Papers, Haynes, I, p. 229.
[1] C. B. P., I, 893, 398; C. B. P., II, 97, 163.
[2] C. S. P., For., 1560-1561, 474; C. B. P., I, 74.
[3] Ibid, 893.
[4] Ibid, 89, 493, 500.

or Council both to the lieutenant and to the wardens.[5] Sometimes even when such direction had been given, the wardens were averse to serving under the Lord Lieutenant and resisted to the point of insubordination. Thus, in 1587, when relations with Scotland were in a critical state by reason of the execution of Mary, Lord Hunsdon wrote to Burghley, saying, "I Perceve yt ys a grete matter too be an Erle," and continues his letter by stating his willingness to lie on the Borders with twenty or thirty men at his own charges, but that he will go to prison before he will serve under Huntingdon,[6] who at that time was Lord Lieutenant of the North. On the shoulders of the Council of the North fell also the task of providing auxiliary militia for border service when on account of the decay in the marches and threatened invasion from Scotland such precaution became necessary.[7]

Finally it was the duty of the President of the Council of the North acting as the Lord Lieutenant to see that the wardens were properly inducted into office, to turn over the court rolls, copies of treaties and other records to the new incumbent,[8] and to act as a court for the investigation of complaints against the warden. The Earl of Huntingdon had the latter duty in the case of Sir John Forster in 1586 and in 1595.[9]

The President of the Council of the North was also given power to appoint a vice-warden in the absence of the warden, but that power seems never to have been exercised.[10]

[5] Ibid, 565, 569, 539. This authority did not extend, however, to dealings with the Scots. C. S. P., Dom., Add., 1566-1579, Eliz. XV, 80.
[6] C. B. P., I, 572.
[7] Ibid, 556, 539; C. B. P., II, 196.
[8] Ibid, 163.
[9] C. B. P., I, 451; C. B. P., II, 163, 197.
[10] Burghley Papers, Haynes, I, p. 229.

CHAPTER IV

BORDER LAW

The law which the wardens enforced in their dealings with disorders in the marches included, besides the authority and directions contained in their commissions and instructions, the treaties with Scotland concerning border matters, and statutes made from time to time which applied to the northern counties. To these we may add certain old customs of the marches and agreements arrived at from time to time by the wardens with the gentlemen of their marches concerning new offences.[1]

There seems to be record of at least four treaties between Elizabeth and the sovereigns of Scotland over border affairs.[2] The records bearing on the subject are somewhat confused, so that it is impossible to say with certainty that there were no others.

Steps toward the first were taken shortly after the signing of the treaty between England and Scotland which had been made in accordance with the peace of Cateau Cambrésis.[3] Commissioners were appointed whe met at Lady Kirke in Scotland, in September, 1559, and agreed upon articles for a treaty concerning border affairs.[4]

Again, on August 4, 1563, Henry, Lord Scrope and Sir John Forster were commissioned to treat with Scotch

---

[1] C. B. P., I, 130.
[2] Ibid, 778; State Papers, Borders, XLI, ff. 238-253; C. B. P., II, 622.
[3] C. S. P., For., 1560-1561, 326.
[4] Sadler State Papers, I, pp. 457-459; C. S. P., For., 1558-1559, 821, 1359.

commissioners regarding border affairs,[5] and a new treaty
was signed September 23, 1563.[6]

Another treaty was made in 1586, which included the
formation of an offensive and defensive alliance between
England and Scotland, and touched upon border matters.
The commission was issued to the Earl of Rutland, Lord
Eure, Mr. Thomas Randolph, and the three wardens, May
31, 1586,[7] and the treaty was signed July 5, 1586.[8] Another treaty is mentioned as having been made the following year,[9] and still another under thirty-six heads was
negotiated in 1597.[10]

Ancient treaties for the borders are sometimes referred
to as being still in force, although war may have broken
out and peace again been declared in the meantime.
Elizabeth, for example, in 1582, wrote to Lord Cesford, a
Scotch warden, telling him that the treaty, made and
agreed upon in the fifth year of Edward VI, ought to be
put in practice.[11]

The occasion for these treaties was the weakness or
total failure of border administration, which led to the appointment of commissioners with fuller authority than
the wardens, whose duty it was to settle by treaty such
matters as the wardens had for any reason been unable to
adjust. In addition, the provisions of former treaties
were reiterated and new provisions to fit new offences
were included.

The treaty of 1563, after arranging for the redress of
complaints which the wardens had not settled, provided

[5] C. S. P., For., 1563, 1103.
[6] Ibid, 1238.
[7] A. P. C., 1586-1587, pp. 135-136.
[8] Rymer, VI, pt. iv, p. 187.
[9] C. B. P., I, 778. This may be the treaty of 1586.
[10] C. B. P., II, 622. Not 1596, as stated in Hodgson's "The Wardens of the Northern Marches."
[11] C. B. P., I, 130.

that the warden himself and not his deputy should hold a
day of truce at least once a month; that they should not
redress value for value or bill for bill, but for all offences
complained of; that the wardens should, at the first day
of truce after the date of the treaty, take, in the presence
of the opposite warden, a solemn oath to execute his office
fully and without partiality. He was to renew the oath
yearly at mid-summer, and a similar oath was to be taken
by all who were called to assist the wardens. The wardens
were to inquire for and to deliver offenders and to 'file'
bills upon their honor or by the oaths of six of their own
wardenry to be named by the opposite warden. Every
one was allowed to follow his lawful trod with hound and
horn, hue and cry and the accustomed manner of fresh
pursuit. The trial of offenders might be made by a lawful assize at the choice of the complainant. Bonds were
to be taken of every lord, owner, possessor or bailiff within
their wardenries that they should bring any of their accused tenants before the wardens at the day of truce to
answer for their offences; if they neglected to so bring the
tenants to the meeting, the lord or possessor or bailiff was to
be punished in place of his tenant, except that he should
not suffer death. Requisitions from the opposite warden
for fugitives were to be honored, and proclamation made
of the fugitives throughout the three marches for six days.
If after that time any should aid the fugitive, the former
was to suffer the punishment unless he was able to find
and bring the latter to the warden. The goods the fugitive
had with him went to the warden of the march where he
was caught if the warden delivered the fugitive to his
opposite. If the fugitive was not delivered, then the goods
in his possession were to go to the warden of the march
from which he fled.

Warners of fugitives were to lose their goods and to
be imprisoned for one year, or to suffer death if both the

English and Scotch wardens thought it proper to inflict
that punishment.

If a person of one country went into the other and
raised a riot and was seized, he was to be treated as a
subject of the realm into which he entered. If he escaped
seizure and returned to his own country he was to be accused, and if found guilty was to be delivered to the
offended warden.

The wardens were permitted to follow offenders into
the opposite realm until they should be taken. Any one
interfering with such pursuit might be complained of.
The pursuer, however, was to give notice of the occasion
of his pursuit to the first person he met and to require his
assistance. Any injury or harm resulting from such pursuit was to be punished by a jury of twelve men of the
country of the one complained of, to be named by the
opposite warden.

The value of cattle was set down at a fixed price to
prevent perjury by either the aggrieved or accused
party.[12] If any one should sow corn in the opposite realm,
he was to forfeit his corn to the complainant, to pay four
times the value of it as a fine and to endure three months
imprisonment. The warden or owner of the ground was
permitted to have for his own use all cattle belonging to
the opposite nation and pastured on his march for six
hours; the offence was to be proven by the testimony of
four witnesses. If, however, the cattle remained for less
than six hours a fine was inflicted.

Any offender found guilty was to be delivered at the day
of truce and if he fled he was to be punished by death as the
breaker of the assurance. If any offender refused to pay

[12] Every ox above four years old was valued at forty shillings;
every cow above four years old, thirty shillings; an ox or a cow
between two and four years old, twenty shillings; an old sheep at
six shillings and a sheep-hog at three shillings and other animals
in the same proportion. State Papers, Borders, XLI, f. 238.

his promised ransom or, failing to pay, refused to reënter as a lawful prisoner he was to be punished according to March Law. A book of the treaties was to be made and published each year at the first day of truce after mid-summer (June 24). A proposition was also made to divide the debatable ground in the East and Middle Marches, and finally, it was provided that all the wardens should use one uniform manner and order of proceeding.[13]

In the memorandum of the Treaty of 1586,[14] besides the provisions for an offensive and defensive alliance between the two realms, there is a provision that all former treaties are to remain in force, although they may seem to have grown out of use. The only new matters connected with the border affairs concerned the action to be taken in case an Englishman was murdered in Scotland; whether a letter of a Scotchman accusing another Scotchman was as good as an advowry,[15] and such minor details of procedure.[16]

The treaty of 1597 contained nothing new regarding border matters, excepting a clause providing for the more severe punishment of blackmailing, both of the giver and receiver.[17] The work of the commission that negotiated this treaty was confined chiefly to the settling of an accumulation of unadjusted disputes between the wardens

[13] Ibid; Rymer, VI, pt. iv, pp, 120-122.

[14] The date in the State Papers is 1585, but it does not seem possible for this to be correct. There is no other reference to a treaty in this year. In State Papers, Borders, XXVII, f. 193, there is a list of treaties in which the treaty of alliance is stated to have been made in 1586, and the treaty of March Law in 1587.

[15] By march customs, a Scot might openly avow on a day of truce that another Scot had committed a crime of which he was charged by an Englishman. This was called an advowry. Owing to the feuds caused thereby, the custom was supplanted by that of the warden filing on his honor, after making secret inquiry. C. B. P., II, 494; C. B. P., I, 171.

[16] State Papers, Borders, XLI, 1543.

[17] C. B. P., II, 622; Rymer, VI, pt. iv, p. 185.

of the two kingdoms, most of them involving questions
of murder. The treaty further provided that old complaints not brought before the commission should be put
to oblivion.[18]

In the treaties made before Elizabeth's time, the provisions of which were continued by the later treaties, are
articles which give a further idea of the sort of offences
which were common in the borders. For example, murderers, thieves, and other offenders fleeing into the opposite kingdom, were not to be received but were to be delivered in ten days after requisition was made. Murderers were to be brought to the day of truce to be tried
and on conviction were to be delivered to the complaining
warden and executed;[19] the damage of a wound was to be
assessed by twelve gentlemen of England and Scotland,
and the giver of the wound was to be delivered to the complaining warden to be imprisoned until he paid double
damages;[20] the receiver of many wounds was to be recom-
pensed in the same way and the offender was besides to
suffer six months' imprisonment. A like arrangement was
made for the assessment of damages growing out of
the burning of houses, or hay or corn in stacks, except
that the offender was to pay all the damages with double
and sawfey.[21] Baughling or raising a disturbance at days
of truce was to be punished by one month's imprisonment.
The valuing of stolen cattle at too high a rate was to be
corrected by an assize.[22] Owners of land could impound
Scotchmen's cattle pasturing there until the owners of the
cattle paid a penny sterling for every nolt and a penny
Scotch (an English farthing) for every sheep. For the

[18] C. B. P., II, 1101, 1137.
[19] State Papers, Borders, XLI, 1543; Treaty of Henry VII.
[20] Treaty of Henry VII; Treaty of Queen Mary.
[21] "With sawfey" meant triple damage. Simple damage was once
the value; double, was twice the value; sawfey increased the fine
once again by the amount of damage. C. B. P., II, 1310.
[22] State Papers, Borders, XLI, 1543.

second offence the fine was to be doubled, and tripled for
the third, and so on till it became two shillings for a nolt
and six-pence for a sheep, whereupon the amount of the
fine went back to the original figure, and the progressive
raising of it went forward again.[23] Hunting in the opposite march was forbidden without the consent of the
owner,[24] nor was timber to be cut without similar permission,[25] though later this permission seems to have been
granted by the warden.[26]

If the warden was unable to deliver an offender, another
person that the warden considered sufficient for the damages claimed was to be delivered. For the third offence
against any of the provisions of the treaty the offender
was to lose his life, providing the second offence was committed after his conviction for the first, and the third after
his conviction for the second.[27] In connection with the
treaties, it is of some interest to find that an undated
paper of the time of Elizabeth gives as one of the causes
of border troubles the fact that the treaties were not understood because they were written in Latin.[28]

The treaties do not, however, give an altogether clear
idea of the actual practice with respect to the punishment
of offences. It frequently happened that a warden would
make an agreement with his opposite warden to adopt a
procedure which was either at variance with, or not ordered by the provisions of a treaty. For example, in
1561, Lord Dacre, Lord Warden of the West March of
England, agreed with Sir John Maxwell, Lord Warden of
the West March of Scotland, to redress for twenty bills,
all to be made of the value of twenty pounds, and to de-

23 State Papers, Borders, XLI, 1543; Treaty of Queen Mary.
24 Treaty of Queen Mary; Treaty of Edward IV.
25 Treaty of Edward IV; Treaty of Henry VIII.
26 Cary's Memoirs, pp. 110-111; C. B. P., II, 988.
27 State Papers, Borders, XLI, 1543.
28 Cott. Ms., Calig. D. I, f. 247.

liver single value for all raids made before September 20, 1560, and triple value for all made since that date.[29] Again, in 1593, Lord Scrope asked Lord Maxwell if they should enter into a thorough redress or make a selection and cast the rest to oblivion.[30] The treaties, however, provided that all offences should be punished and they do not provide a choice of punishments to be determined by the chronological order of the offences. After the division of the Debatable Lands, the dwellers there constantly shifted their allegiance from one country to the other in order to escape punishment. If the Scotch warden was active they were Englishmen; if the English warden pursued them, they claimed to be subjects of Scotland. In 1573, therefore, Lord Scrope and Lord Herries agreed to try to settle the trouble by each holding court the same day in the late Debatable Lands in the name of their respective sovereigns.[31] No method of determining the allegiance of the Graemes was provided either in the treaties or the instructions of the wardens and this step must have been taken upon the warden's general authority.

There are not to be found among the statutes many which relate particularly and solely to border administration.

Neither Elizabeth or her predecessors had ever been granted by parliament any right to appoint wardens nor to clothe them with such extensive powers as we find them to have. It is easy, therefore, to accept the statement of Lord Eure to Burghley that the border laws were derived from the accustomed laws of a camp[32] and to look for their justification in the fact that the wardens were military rather than civil officers.

[29] C. S. P., For., 1561-1562, 431.
[30] C. B. P., I, 885.
[31] C. S. P., For., 1572-1574, 866.
[32] C. B. P., II, 469.

From time to time, however, statutes were passed by
parliament which applied either specifically or by impli-
cation to the three northern counties. On the other
hand, in some cases the border counties are especially exempted from the operation of the law.

It has been impossible exactly to determine whether
these laws were always, as they certainly were in some
instances, enforced by the wardens rather than by the
civil authority.

One of the earliest laws applying to the marches of
which there is record is that of Richard II, Chapter 16,
which provided that no armor or victuals or other re-
freshment should pass into Scotland without license of
the king on pain of forfeiture thereof, one-third of which
was to go to the informer.[33]

From another statute, passed in the reign of Henry
VI,[34] it appears that the wardens had been unduly extending their authority. The law states that attachments
by the warden had been unduly extended out of the counties of York, Northumberland, Cumberland and Westmorland, and provided that resistance to such attachments
was lawful, that the parties aggrieved should have triple
damages and that the defendant was to suffer two years'
imprisonment and to pay a fine of one hundred shillings
to the king. Furthermore, Justices of the Peace, Sheriffs
and Stewards of Leets might enquire thereof.[35]

The troubles of the wardens were doubtless much increased by the facility with which munitions, food supplies
and other contraband could be carried across the border
into or from Scotland under the guise of ordinary com-
merce. With the object of regulating the traffic an act
was passed in the reign of Edward IV,[36] having for its

[33] Statutes of the Realm, II, p. 35.
[34] 31 Henry VI, Chapter 3.
[35] Statutes of the Realm, II, p. 363.
[36] 22 Edward IV, Chapter 8.

title "An Act for the Safety of Berwick and the
Marches." This provided that all merchandise passing
from Scotland and the Isles to England, Ireland and
Wales or vice versa was to be customed at either Berwick
or Carlisle.[37] In 1576, it was ordered that this act be
proclaimed on the borders and searchers put on the fron-
tiers,[38] and as late as 1602, the wardens were given especial command to enforce it.[39]

The statute 7 Henry VII, Chapter 6, provided that
Scotchmen were to be driven out of England within forty
days after proclamation on pain of forfeiture of goods and
chattels and imprisonment of their persons. Constables
who refused or neglected to enforce this statute were to
be fined twenty shillings.[40]

In the time of Henry VIII, two acts were passed forbidding the export of horses into Scotland under penalty
of the forfeiture of the value of the horse, the informer
to get one-half. The wardens and justices of the peace
were given authority to enquire into and punish offences
against the act.[41] This act seems to have been repealed
by the general terms of acts passed in the reigns of Edward VI, and Philip and Mary, but was reënacted by 1
Elizabeth, Chapter 7, and the enforcement of it turned
over to warden courts and to the justices of the peace in
quarter sessions.[42] Incident to this act we find an example of how the statutes were made known to the inhabitants of the marches. On May 14, 1559, an allowance
was granted to "Rich. Jugge and John Cawode," printers
to the queen, for printing five hundred proclamations of

[37] Statutes of the Realm, II, p. 475.
[38] C. S. P., For., 1575-1577, 930.
[39] C. B. P., II, 1545.
[40] Statutes of the Realm, II, p. 553; C. B. P., II, 213.
[41] 23 Henry VIII, C. 16; 32 Henry VIII, C. 6; Statutes of the
Realm, III, pp. 380, 751.
[42] Ibid, IV, pt. i, p. 367.

the Act of Parliament to revive the statute of 23 Henry VIII, touching the conveyance of horses, etc., in Scotland.[43]

The statute 2 and 3 Philip and Mary, Chapter 1, provided for a commission to enquire into the decay of the castles, towers, and other defences of the borders. These commissioners were either to be residents, or else freeholders having land worth forty pounds per year within twenty miles of Scotland. If not residing within this limit they had to be learned in the law. They had to take oath to well and truly perform their duty and were subject to a penalty of forty pounds if they served illegally. They were commissioned under the great seal, but if any of the liberties and possessions of the Duchy of Lancaster or of the Bishopric of Durham came within the survey of the commissioners, other commissions were to be issued under the seal of the Duchy and of the County Palatine of Durham. If the officers of the Duchy or County Palatine refused to issue a commission within six days, then the commissioners could proceed within the Duchy or County with their commission under the great seal.

The commission had power to compel the attendance of witnesses through sheriffs, bailiffs and other officers. As a result of the testimony of these witnesses the commission could order repairs made, fields enclosed, fords destroyed, and in general could take such steps as they thought necessary to provide for the proper defence of the borders within twenty miles of Scotland. The decrees made by the commissioners were to be certified into chancery and when they received the royal assent, would have the force of law but not unless so certified. They were not to be altered except by act of parliament. In order to enforce their decrees the commissioners could im-

43 C. S. P., For., 1558-1559, 678.

pose any reasonable fines and amercements. The penalties inflicted for disobedience were to be applied to the purposes of the act. The commissioners were not to sell or let land except in cases where it had been forfeited. No fees were to be charged for the issuing of the commission and it was to continue for seven years unless suspended.[44]

The statute 23 Elizabeth, Chapter 4, was a further attempt to remedy the condition of the border defences. It authorized a commission to inquire into the decays on the border, similar to that authorized by 2 and 3 Philip and Mary, Chapter 1, and provided that the charges for making the proper repairs should be levied on the owners anywhere in the realm, and that those on the queen's lands should be paid by the receiver of the county. If the under-tenant was at fault in allowing a place to decay contrary to his lease the cost of repairs had to be borne by him. A method for the renewal of the covenant for border service[45] was provided for in cases where it had been allowed to fall into disuse. All future lessees of lands were to be resident within their leaseholds, but lords were not to be interfered with if the tenant was furnished. The statute was to continue for the term of her majesty's life, and that of 2 and 3 Philip and Mary, Chapter 1, was extended for twenty years and then to the end of the parliament next ensuing.[46] Sir John Forster writing to

[44] Statutes of the Realm, IV, pt. i, pp. 266-269.
[45] "All the inhabitants of the Borders are bownd wthout taking any wages to assemble at the W. or his deputyes call for the resistance of invasion of the enemies though the assemblie dure XX dayes at one time. They are bownd to mayntayn watches as well by day as by night, . . . They are bownd to mayntayne the Becon lites for anempst Scotland & the sea coastes; . . . They are all bownd to ride wth the L. Warden or his Deputye 2 or 3 times in the yeare not tarying in Scotland over one day & 2 nights going & coming at theyr owne expences." State Papers, Borders, XX, 76.
[46] Statutes of the Realm, IV, pt. i, p. 663, et seq.

Burghley in 1592, answered Burghley's question as to
what had been done under this statute by saying that he
remembered only one commission which was to inquire
into decay but that it had done very little and that
many gentlemen had since laid towns waste to make
demesnes.[47]

Still another statute which was made use of for border
purposes was that of 35 Elizabeth, Chapter 4,[48] which
provided for the collection of a sum of money from
each parish for the relief of poor soldiers. Shortly after the
passage of this act, Lord Scrope wrote to Burghley with a
proposition for paying Sir Henry Leigh as Keeper of
Brough Barony without expense to the queen. He suggested using the money collected for hurt soldiers and
mariners, of which there were few chargeable on Cumberland and Westmorland, to pay the expenses of twenty
or thirty horse at Rockcliff Castle during the winter sea-
son.[49]

The giving and receiving of blackmail was an offence
which the wardens strove earnestly to prevent. As far
back as 1559, Sir Ralph Sadler wrote to Sir William Cecil
that in the last wars he heard what he had never heard
before, that to be assured from spoil the English borderers
pay the Scotch certain tributes.[50] This custom was to be
restrained, according to a note of 1568, by proclamation.
The remedy was, however, ineffectual and the situation
seems to have become worse[51] until it was stated that it
would be better for the borders to pay six subsidies in a
year than to pay this unlawful tax.[52] In 1601, Lord
Scrope agreed with the gentlemen of his wardenry to pun-

---

[47] C. B. P., I, 786.
[48] Statutes of the Realm, IV, pt. ii, p. 847.
[49] C. B. P., I, 882, 954.
[50] C. S. P., For., 1558-1559, 1339; Sadler State Papers, II, p. 16.
[51] C. S. P., For., 1566-1568, 2133; C. B. P., II, 119.
[52] Ibid, 431.

ish blackmailing,[53] and, finally, by the statute of 43
Elizabeth, Chapter 13, taking or paying blackmail, carrying or detaining a person against his will or aiding or
abetting therein, or burning stacks of corn, were made
felonies without benefit of clergy. The new law was to be
proclaimed by the sheriffs at Carlisle, Penrith and Cock-
ermouth in Cumberland; at Appleby and Kendal in Westmorland; in Newcastle-upon-Tyne; at Morpeth, Alnwick
and Hexham in Northumberland; at Durham, Darlington,
Bishop Aucklands and Barnard Castle in Durham; and
at Berwick-upon-Tweed. Mayors and other officers were
to make like proclamations at fairs and at every six-weeks'
market.[54]

Early in the reign of Elizabeth, subsidies appear to have
been collected from the borders as from the other counties
of England,[55] but in a letter written by Sir John Forster,
in 1575, he suggests that the borderers be not charged with
the payment of such taxes in consideration of their other
services.[56] The suggestion was already a part of Elizabeth's plan for the government of the borders, for in all
the statutes passed during the reign of Elizabeth granting
subsidies, and fifteenths and tenths for the augmentation
of the royal revenues, the inhabitants of the marches, in
return for their liability for border service, were exempted
from the payment of the tax.[57] The wardens were also
expressly excluded from the operation of the law of 14
Elizabeth, Chapter 5, the act for the punishment of vaga-
bonds, etc. This act provides for the granting of licenses
to beg and pass from shire to shire by the justices of the

53 Ibid, 1192.
54 Statutes of the Realm, IV, pt. ii, pp. 979-981.
55 C. S. P., For., 1558-1559, 1140.
56 Ibid, 1575-1577, 167.
57 8 Elizabeth, C. 18; 23 Eliz., C. 15; 27 Eliz., C. 29; 29 Eliz.,
C. 8; 31 Eliz., C. 15; 35 Eliz., C. 13; 39 Eliz., C. 27; 43 Eliz., C.
18; Statutes of the Realm, IV, pt. i, pp. 505, 684, 744; pt. ii, pp.
778, 818, 867, 937, 991.

peace, and forbids their being granted by others, but it also states that the rights of the wardens of the three marches toward Scotland and the captains of Berwick and Carlisle to grant passports or safe-conducts is not to be interfered with.[58]

It is not clear whether the statute of 7 Edward VI, Chapter 65, applied to the marches or not, but if it did, it certainly was not enforced. This was an act for the regulation of taverns and ale houses in England, and provided that there should be forty in London, four in Newcastle-upon-Tyne, and not above two in any other town.[59] The marches are not excepted from the operation of the statute, but in a report dated 1577, Berwick is named as having seventy-four, the East March one hundred thirty-seven and the Middle March, one hundred twenty-three.[60] This seems to be a disproportionate number, for in a census taken in 1565, Berwick had but 3,511 inhabitants,[61] and in 1570, Lord Hunsdon estimates 6,000 or 7,000 people to be in the town.[62] Other acts which spread over the northern counties appear not to have affected their military administration.

There are several drafts of acts, however, for the better regulation of the borders which do not appear to have been made into statutes. One, for example, proposed in 1581, provided that in order to clear ambiguities in the unwritten laws which vary in the several marches, twenty-eight different offences should be made march treason, of which four were to be punishable by death, and none of the twenty-eight were to have benefit of clergy.[63] Another, drafted in 1596, recited the fact that the inhabitants of the

[58] Statutes of the Realm, IV, pt. i, p. 592.
[59] Ibid, 169.
[60] State Papers, Borders, XX, f. 18.
[61] C. S. P., For., 1564-1565, 1232.
[62] Ibid, 1569-1571, 1153.
[63] C. B. P., I, 81.

four northern countries are freed from the payment of
subsidies and so are bound to defend the frontier at their
own charges; that tenants who held on low rent and
by an ancient custom called tenant right are now decayed
and unable, and that, on the other hand, landlords are
laying lands in pasture in large farms and suppressing
small holdings; that they lease their lands to Scots, and
that they oppress their English tenants by heavy fines for
renewals, and that some of the worst offenders are the
queen's tenants-in-chief. The act, therefore, proposed
that a commission should be formed, of which six were to
be of the *quorum*, which was to have full power to redress all decays and defaults.[64]

With the union of the kingdoms the administration of
the borders was rapidly simplified. Shortly after his
accession, James issued a proclamation looking to the better administration of justice through the ordinary civil
courts in what he called "The Middle Shires," and in
1605, he issued another proclamation providing that a
special commission of an equal number of English and
Scotch should have power to hear and determine all border troubles according to the laws of the marches, thus
doing away with government by wardens.[65] Lord William
Howard, the "Belted Will of Scott's *Marmion*, was
one of these commissioners, but was not, as is sometimes
stated, at any time a warden.

Following this proclamation by a few years there are
two statutes dealing with what had been the borders.
The first, passed in 1607, provided for the general repeal
of all acts which interfered with free traffic and communi-
cation between the English and the Scotch; that none was
to be prosecuted under border laws for offences committed

[64] C. B. P., II, 462.
[65] Rymer, VII, pt. ii, p. 129.

62 BORDER LAW

prior to the death of Elizabeth, and further provided that offenders should be tried by ordinary law and in their own country.[66] The second, passed in 1610, provided for the extradition of offenders to the country in which the crime had been committed.[67]

[66] 4 James I, C. 1; Statutes of the Realm, IV, pt. ii, pp. 1134-1137.

[67] 7 James I, C. 1; Statutes of the Realm, IV, pt. ii, p. 1157.

CHAPTER V

DAYS OF TRUCE

As has been previously stated, two of the chief administrative duties of the wardens were the keeping of Days of
Truce with their opposite wardens of Scotland, and the
holding of Warden Courts.

The day of truce was a day fixed by agreement between
an English warden and the opposite warden of Scotland
upon which the respective wardens and their followers
met at some point at or near the boundary for mutual redress of grievances and complaints. It was the customary
method by which satisfaction was obtained for injuries by
subjects of the opposite realm. As its proper and orderly keeping was of importance in maintaining peace on
the borders, we find that directions concerning the frequency and manner of its holding were carefully laid down
in the warden's commission, in the various treaties made
from time to time with Scotland, as well as in notes made
by the wardens of the customs of the borders with respect
to such meetings.[1] The treaties only provided for the
general fact of redress under certain conditions while the
customs of the borders were followed as to the details.

The places at which days of truce were held and which
had been fixed upon by custom were usually in the march
of one of the wardens holding the meeting[2] although the
warden of the English Middle March, which adjoined and
was in constant danger from all three Scotch marches,
met the warden of the East March of Scotland within the
East March of England.

[1] State Papers, Borders, XLI, 1543.
[2] C. B. P., II, 1292; cf. treaties.

63

The common meeting place for the East Marches of England and of Scotland was at the Reddenburn or Rydingburn, a small stream that one can easily step across, which forms part of the boundary between England and Scotland and which empties into the Tweed near Wark Castle.[3] Sometimes, however, the meeting was held at Wark, on the Tweed, or at Coldstream.[4] The meeting place for the East March of England and the Middle March of Scotland was either at Reddenburn[5] or at Etall or Carham in England and at Kelso or Reddan in Scotland.[6]

For the Middle March of England and the East March of Scotland several meeting places are mentioned. One was at the Reddenburn; a second place and the one most often used for meetings was at Staweford,[7] where Bowmont Water crosses the boundary between England and Scotland; still another was at the Cocklaw in the Cheviot Hills.[8] When the wardens met at towns some distance within their marches as sometimes happened in the Middle March, as it also did in the East March, the meeting was generally at Kirkyettan in Scotland and at Kirknewton in England. Liddesdale, in Scotland, had a keeper of its own who would not answer for offences through the Scotch wardens. The Warden of the Middle March met the Keeper of Liddesdale for redress at Kemelspeth.[9]

For the settling of complaints between the Middle March of England and the Middle March of Scotland, the usual meeting places were Kirkyettan and Kirknewton, though

[3] C. S. P., For., 1569-1571, 471.
[4] C. B. P., II, 993; C. S. P., For., 1564-1565, 408.
[5] Ibid, 1560-1561, 1001.
[6] C. B. P., II, 1002; 1094.
[7] C. B. P., I, 305, 702.
[8] C. B. P., II, 993.
[9] C. B. P., I, 115.

sometimes meetings were held at Jedburgh, Kelso, Alnwick and Hexpethgatehead.[10]

The Warden of the West March usually met his opposite at Gretna Church, though a place called Tordowath is also named.[11] When this warden dealt with Liddlesdale, however, the accustomed place was at Kershope Foot where Kershope Burn empties into Liddel Water.[12] Lord Scrope once refused to meet Cesford, the Keeper of Liddesdale, at Kemelspeth as that was the meeting place for the Middle March and was never used by him or his predecessors.[13]

The accumulation of offences rather than the provisions of treaties determined the frequency with which such days of truce should be held. According to the latter the days of truce were to be held once each month or oftener.[14] This requirement appears, however, to have been more honored in the breach than in the observance,[15] and we find many complaints from both Scotch and English that the monthly meetings required by the treaties were not held.

When an English warden desired to hold a day of truce he sent his clerk to the Scotch warden with a proposition to meet at certain places, one in England and one in Scotland, on a certain day or days.[16] The place named for each march was not always the same but was one of two or three places where such meetings were customarily held.

The treaties provided that all offences should be re-

---

[10] C. S. P., For., 1561-1562, 939; C. B. P., 421.
[11] Ibid, 106, 777; C. B. P., II, 502.
[12] C. B. P., I, 106.
[13] Ibid. The more important places of meeting have been marked on the map.
[14] C. B. P., II, 46.
[15] C. B. P., I, 676, 685.
[16] C. B. P., I, 105, 765.

dressed, but in the correspondence arranging for the meeting it was customary for the two wardens to decide whether all offences should be settled;[17] or whether a Scotch complaint against England should be balanced by an English complaint against Scotland;[18] or, finally, whether the value of the Scotch complaints against England should be balanced by an equal value of English complaints against Scotland.[19] The last two methods seem to have been the more common. Had the settlement been made as provided in the treaty, one or the other nation would have been the debtor for which hostages would have to be given. The answering of one bill by another is more frequent, since the amounts owing by the offenders of the two nations were apt to be more nearly equal, and besides the warden whose march had committed the fewest wrongs might find it necessary to consent to such an arrangement in order to get any redress at all. On the other hand a warden often objected to meeting bill with bill. For example, on one occasion, Lord Scrope urged Burghley not to agree that the Scotch wardens should be permitted to do so, since a bill of one thousand pounds would be answered by one of twenty pounds.[20]

The arrangements for the day of truce having been fixed by correspondence, each warden proclaimed at several places within his march[21] that a day of truce would be held on a certain date. At the same time, a proclamation was made that all those in his wardenry who had any complaints to make against the Scotch should present their grievances to the warden or one of his serjeants at one or

17 Ibid, 105, 499, 685, etc.
18 C. B. P., II, 1410.
19 C. B. P., I, 183.
20 C. B. P., II, 369.
21 State Papers, Borders, XLI, ff. 238-253, passim.

more places within the march on a day which generally
preceded the date of the day of truce by a few weeks.[22]

These complaints were enrolled and a copy sent to the
Scotch warden. At this point one of two methods of procedure was followed. Sometimes the opposite warden
after receiving the list sent back to the English warden a
list of the bills he would answer for, apparently after having made inquiry and being satisfied as to the truth of
the complaints.[23] If this method was followed, the only
business of the day of truce was the delivery of offenders
on both sides. The more usual method, however, was for
the trial itself as well as the delivery of offenders to take
place on the day of truce.

The preliminary matters having been settled,[24] the warden issued a second proclamation in the name of the
queen to all lords, knights, esquires, gentlemen, and officers requiring them on a certain day to attend the warden
at his residence with a suitable number of their tenants
and servants. All were to be mounted on their best horses
and armed as completely as possible. The company assembled on the evening previous to the day of truce. The
next morning the warden with his company rode to the
march or boundary between the realms. Then the warden
of England, having learned that the Scotch warden had
also come to the place of meeting, sent his deputy or some
other gentleman with others of his company to the Scotch
warden to beg assurance for the safety of his men during
the meeting and until sunrise of the next day. A like as-

---

[22] The account of the method of holding a day of truce is given
from the English standpoint. The Scotch warden went through the
same procedure.

[23] C. B. P., I, 788.

[24] A full account of the method of procedure at a day of truce is
given in State Papers, Borders, XLI, ff. 238-253.

surance was required by the Scotch warden from the English.[25] This assurance having been mutually given both wardens made proclamation among their attendants for the preservation of the peace from the time of making the proclamation until the next day at sunrise on pain of death. The English warden with his company then entered Scotland where the Scotch warden awaited his coming. After meeting and holding some conference with each other, the wardens withdrew somewhat apart from their companies and proceeded with their clerks to call the rolls of bills for both sides.[26]

The custom of the English warden taking the initiative of going into Scotland arose from the killing, in a previous reign, of a Scotch warden by the attendants of the English warden.[27] The English wardens seem in this case to have made a virtue of a necessity, for on entering Scotland it was the custom for the warden to proclaim, "I will loose the Kinge [or Queen] my master no grounde."[28] Toward the close of the reign of Elizabeth, however, this custom was changed, perhaps owing to the unfortunate killing of Lord Russell, the son-in-law of Sir John Forster, in a meeting between Forster and Lord Ker of Fernihurst. In 1598, Robert Cary wrote to Cecil to say that the best English borderers said that the first meeting of the wardens was always in mid-stream[29] when the boundary was a river or other water; and, in 1599, Sir Robert Ker and Willoughby cast lots to determine who should be the first

[25] The assurance of peace was understood to be for as long as the business should require, though nominally to last only till sunrise of the following day. C. B. P., II, 283.
[26] State Papers, Borders, XLI, 1543. A copy of a short roll of bills giving their general form will be found in Appendix B.
[27] C. B. P., II, 1134.
[28] Ibid, 1001.
[29] Ibid, 909.

to satisfy complaints, in which instance Willoughby won
and Sir Robert came into England and delivered his offenders first.[30]

If any doubt arose during the calling of the bills as to
whether those charged with offences were guilty or not,
then the bill was to be tried either by the warden's honor,
or by an assize of twelve gentlemen, six from England to
be named by the Scotch warden and six from Scotland to
be named by the English warden, or by an avower. So
many feuds, however, arose from the latter custom that it
was changed to a negative form. The person accused and
four or six others could swear that he was innocent of the
crime charged.[31] The filing on the honor of the warden
was another effort to avoid the feuds that resulted from
one Scot avowing that another was guilty of a crime.
When the warden filed on his honor he was supposed to investigate the charges when the bills were received from the
opposite warden and to state on his honor that the person
accused was innocent or guilty.[32] The custom seems to
have become less and less common toward the end of Elizabeth's reign,[33] and the method of trial to have taken its
place.

The assizers, as well as those selected to excuse bills in
the absence of an avower, were to be sworn to render a
true decision. The aggrieved persons were also sworn to
make a true statement of what their goods were worth at
the time they were taken, that they knew no other remedy
and that the goods were all taken at one time.[34] This practice was the occasion of much perjury. To correct this
evil the treaty made in 1563 fixed a list of prices for

[30] Ibid, 1094.
[31] State Papers, Borders, XLI, 1543.
[32] C. B. P., I, 676.
[33] C. B. P., II, 187.
[34] Ibid, 1090; State Papers, Borders, XLI, 1543.

cattle which should not be exceeded in making claims for damages.[35]

The business of the day also included the delivery of offenders found guilty and the payment of damages. The wardens were to deliver offenders within fifteen days under penalty of ten pounds for each month they remained undelivered.[36] We have also seen that in case the offender could not be delivered it was the custom of the warden to deliver some one of equal responsibility in his place. These pledges were, in England, sent usually to York to be imprisoned until satisfaction was made[37] and were supported by that portion of the Scotch march for which they were pledged.[38] Much trouble arose from this custom since there was great difficulty in securing the money, not only for their release but even for their support while in jail.[39] Furthermore, it appears that their escape from jail released those for whom they were bound from paying any damages.[40] On being bound the pledges had to be spoken to individually, as follows: "Lard of Overton, you are to answer for your selfe and surname so muche" or else suffer penalty [of death] before the year is out.[41]

In spite of this rather elaborate provision for securing the punishment of alien offenders, there is much complaint of the ineffectiveness of the day of truce as a means of obtaining justice.

One of the causes of its failure was the lack of authority of the Scotch wardens over the inhabitants of their marches. These had, for example, no authority over Liddesdale, whose inhabitants were constantly complained of

[35] Rymer, VI, pt. iv, pp. 120-122.
[36] Nicholson's Leges Marchiarum, p. 188.
[37] C. B. P., II, 1166; State Papers, Borders, XXXIV, f. 301.
[38] C. B. P., II, 1166, 1041.
[39] Ibid, 1416.
[40] Ibid, 1266, 1049; C. S. P., For., 1572-1574, 19.
[41] Ibid, 1045.

by the English as the worst offenders.[42] This district nominally had a Keeper who was responsible to the King for
its good order. Usually, however, the Keeper of Liddesdale was one of the powerful Scotch border nobles that
James could neither coax nor coerce into doing justice.[43]
Thus, Lord Scrope, in 1592, wrote to Burghley, "It maie
please your good Lp. farder to be informed that during
these xiiii yeares last past there hathe bene not anie re-
dresse answered for Lyddis Dale."[44]

Another trouble which interfered with the effectiveness
of the day of truce was the difficulty of obtaining redress
from the Scotch wardens for offences committed prior to
the dates of their commissions.[45] As the strength of the
parties in Scotland shifted from time to time this became
a serious matter to the English warden. For example,
Scrope wrote to Cecil in January, 1600, that this frequent
exchange of officers in Scotland prevented redress.[46] A
similar complaint of disobedience is made by a Scotch
warden, Lord Ker of Cesford, concerning Teviotdale or
"Tevydale" as an excuse for not giving justice to the
English.[47] In despair the English wardens instead of
dealing with the Scotch wardens adopted the expedient of
taking bonds from the chiefs of surnames not to commit
spoilings in England.[48]

Another interference with the securing of justice at the
meeting of the wardens was the refusal of the Scotch
wardens to answer for injuries or murders. In some cases,
it was claimed that this refusal was by the order of James
to his wardens or by arrangement between the sovereigns

[42] C. B. P., I., 40, 167, 409, 676, 745, etc.
[43] C. B. P., II, 187, 1398.
[44] State Papers, Borders, XXVII, f. 106; C. S. P., Dom., Add.,
1580-1625, Eliz. XXXII, 39.
[45] C. B. P., I., 282.
[46] C. B. P., II, 1143.
[47] C. B. P., I, 167, 992.
[48] C. B. P., I, 70.

pending the appointment of commissioners.[49]　When the
Scotch wardens refused to settle for hurts the English
wardens generally declined to meet them at all.[50]

Still another difficulty was due to what was called the
'shooting' of meetings. This custom, by no means so vio-
lent as it sounds, was that of a warden refusing for one
cause or another to keep the day of truce after it had been
appointed by agreement with his opposite.[51] Numerous
complaints against the Scotch wardens were sent by the
English wardens to the Privy Council on account of this
custom, though it was not confined to Scotland. For example, Sir John Forster, in 1587, refused on account of
the execution of Mary to keep an appointment for a day
of truce that he had made with Lord Cesford, and Robert
Cary refused to keep a like appointment in 1598.[52]

The raising of a disturbance or a fray at a day of truce
often prevented the securing of justice at the meeting.
Occasionally the results were so disturbing that the only
solution was through a meeting of English and Scotch
commissioners, who settled the matter by treaty.

In one instance a group of English who were following the fray passed near the meeting place. The assembly promptly broke up to enable the English present to
join their fellow-countrymen. John Cary in writing to
Cecil about the affair said that they would have gotten all
their justice if it hadn't been for that.[53]

Another disturbing custom was that of 'baughling' or
'bawlching.' This was the carrying around on a spear of
the glove or coat of a person who had been convicted of an
offence and had been bound for damages but who had not
kept the pledge. The act was an accusation that he had

49 Ibid, 117, 127, 129, 164, 206, 241; C. B. P., II, 209.
50 C. B. P., I, 129.
51 Ibid, 123, 190, 204, 473, 691, etc.
52 Ibid, 485; C. B. P., II, 561.
53 C. B. P., II, 1485.

broken his faith and usually resulted in an immediate fight.[54] Baughling at a day of truce was punished by fine and imprisonment but the custom seems to have kept up as long as truce days were held.

More important in their results than these minor affrays were the disturbances which resulted in the murder of gentlemen on either side. Two such affairs occurred within the reign of Elizabeth. The first was the killing of Sir George Heron and fifteen other Englishmen at a day of truce held at Redeswier in July, 1575, between Sir John Forster and the Keeper of Liddesdale. Sir John Forster, the warden, was taken prisoner and kept in ward by the Scotch for nearly three weeks. The Regent of Scotland was willing to make almost any amends for this act, even offering Carmichael, the Scotch warden, as hostage to the queen. The final result was, however, not altogether satisfactory to the English. Eight Scots were sent to England to pay the penalty for the crime, but Lord Hunsdon said of them that they were a "sort of beggarly Harlotts and sheep thieves" and not worth hanging.[55] In a report made just after the affair happened, it was stated that it was partly the Englishmen's own fault for it was against the ancient custom for a warden to meet a keeper.[56]

The second affair was the killing of Sir Francis Russell by a chance shot in an affray raised at a truce day held between Sir John Forster and Lord Ker of Fernihurst. The Privy Council seems to have thought that Forster was at fault in this case, for the state papers are full of explanations from the wardens and other borderers concerning the manner of holding a day of truce.[57] The

[54] C. B. P., I, 329, C. B. P., II, 783, 784, 907, 1310.
[55] C. S. P., For., 1575-1577, 215, 216, 244, 257, 283, 297, 352.
[56] Ibid, 309.
[57] Cott. Ms. Calig., C. VIII, f. 199, et seq; C. B. P., I, 330, et seq.; Letters of Elizabeth and James, Cam. Soc. Pub., vol. 79, pp. 18, 19, 20, 27, 31, etc.

death of Lord Russell occurred in July, 1585, and was the
immediate cause of the appointment of commissioners and
the treaty concerning the borders which was made early
in 1586, at which meeting Sir Thomas Ker was convicted
for complicity in this offence. He was imprisoned at
Aberdeen as a punishment, where he died the same year.[58]

A more summary method of securing redress than that
provided by the day of truce was the custom known as
"following the trod." Trod or "troade" was of two sorts,
"hot" which was fresh pursuit when the goods were stolen,
and "cold," which was pursuit at any other time there-
after. When following the trod the pursuers could pass
into the opposite realm. If this occurred the pursuer had
to take witness of the first person he met or of the residents of the first village he came to that he was on lawful
trod; he was also required to ask their company and assistance in that pursuit. "Troublance of trod" was the
expression used to describe assaults upon or interference
with the lawful pursuer of a trod. The treaties provided
that the trod should be made openly with hue and cry
and hound and horn. When the offender was caught he
was described as having been taken with the red hand and
summary vengeance might be taken upon him,[59] even to
the extent of taking his life and burning his house.[60]

A curious means of getting assistance in the following of
the trod is indicated in a complaint of the Rutledges' to
Walsingham. Their brother had been hurt and they had
gone to Lord Scrope, the warden, and had shown him "the
bloody shirt" and required his assistance with men. Lord
Scrope neglected to aid them and their brother was afterwards murdered by the same persons who had earlier injured him.[61]

[58] C. B. P., I, 417.
[59] C. B. P., II, 1310.
[60] C. S. P., For., 1572-1574, 115.
[61] C. B. P., I, 191.

The difficulty of securing complete redress at a day of truce has already been referred to. As the cases accumulated in which justice could not be secured, the complaints to the queen and the Privy Council increased in number until the Council was moved to devise a remedy. This remedy usually took the form of a commission which was to meet a similar commission from Scotland to settle all disputed questions. There is, for example, the statement that when the wardens stop justice for private causes, the sovereigns appointed some special man to join with these officers to further justice.[62] Again, in 1580, Lord Scrope stated that he understood that the Scotch King had appointed commissioners to meet the border wardens at Berwick to redress complaints.[63]

The commissioners were usually the same as those which negotiated the treaties made from time to time and which have already been mentioned in the first part of this chapter. At their meeting the commissioners decided what raids should be redressed and in what order; the method for the trial of particular cases was arranged; and, in general, they tried to clear away all disputes. For example, in 1559, after filing the bills, the commissioners set a time for delivery of all offenders and ordered the wardens to keep their days of truce at the appointed places in each march and at frequent times, that to avoid trouble the warden should file and deliver on honor, and further provided that prisoners should be honestly treated and charitably housed in time to come.[64]

A few years later, in 1563, there is a record of another commission.[65] After 1563, however, we do not find a record of any other until 1585-1586. The long interval may

[62] C. B. P., II, 342, 400.
[63] C. B. P., I, 49.
[64] Sadler State Papers, I, p. 459.
[65] C. B. P., I, 57.

be accounted for by the fact that during the first ten
years of Elizabeth's reign, many other difficulties in the
relationship between Scotland and England had to be
settled and border affairs were neglected, while the merci-
less punishment visited on both the Scotch and English
adherents of the Rising in the North was a lesson which
lasted for a number of years. As early as 1580, there
were tentative arrangements for the appointment of a new
commission.[66] The actual work of this commission was,
according to Sir John Forster, to secure a general redress
on both sides since 1563.[67] The meeting appears to have
been delayed from time to time for one cause or another.
Finally, in 1585, they came together, but the Scotch commissioners refused to allow delivery either for murder or
breach of the truce.[68] A treaty was, however, made, and
as we have previously noted, Sir Thomas Ker was convicted for his responsibility for the murder of Lord Russell.

In 1588, another commission was appointed by Lord
Hunsdon under authorization by the queen.[69] The commission met early in the year and filed many of the largest
bills on both sides and provided for the delivery of pledges
to the wardens who were to appoint days to make delivery
for eighty other bills.[70] The commissioners evidently
dealt with the larger and more important bills but used
their authority to force the settlement of the smaller ones
by the wardens. The commissioners further ordained that
all attempts since Haldenrigg (1570) should be redressed
and that proclamation to that effect should be made at

[66] Ibid, 56. In 1577, Maxwell wrote to Lord Scrope saying that
there had not been one attempt in six months. C. S. P., For., 1575-
1577, 1384.
[67] C. B. P., I, 57.
[68] C. B. P., I, 171.
[69] Ibid, 585, 586.
[70] Ibid, 587, 588.

Berwick, Alnwick, Morpeth, Hexham, Carlisle, Burton and other needful places.[71]

Another commission was appointed late in 1595; [72] the immediate cause of this was the rescue of Kinmont Willie from Carlisle Castle by Buccleugh, and the arrest of Roger Woodrington, a deputy warden of the Middle March, by Sir Robert Ker, a Scotch warden. William Armstrong of Kinmont had, it was claimed, broken the truce on a day of meeting between the Scots and the English. He was taken by some of Lord Scrope's retinue and imprisoned in Carlisle Castle on March 17, 1596. Four weeks later, on the stormy night of April 14, Walter Scott of Hardyng (an ancestor of Sir Walter Scott), Will of Rosetrees and Ritchie's Hutcheon, with five hundred other of Buccleugh's friends, armed and provided with crow-bars, picks, axes, and scaling ladders, undermined the postern door of the outer ward of the castle, got to the room where Kinmont was imprisoned, released him, and escaped before they were seen by the watch of the inner ward. The offence made Lord Scrope furious with anger and chagrin and he refused to have anything to do with the Scots, either to give redress or to secure it, until some satisfaction was given him for this invasion of the castle of which he was the keeper. Woodrington, the deputy warden, was simply seized in revenge for the taking of Kinmont.[73] Besides these offences, claims of a total value of nearly one hundred thousand pounds sterling stood unredressed.[74]

In a letter written to Lord Burghley by William Bowes there is an interesting account of the procedure of the commission. Two of the commissioners and two deputy

---

[71] Ibid, 582, 593, 594.
[72] C. B. P., II, 179.
[73] C. B. P., II, 237, 252, 257, 264, 274, 285, etc.
[74] Ibid, 485; Letters of Elizabeth and James, Cam. Soc. Pub., Vol. 79, p. 114.

wardens settled Scotch bills. At the same time the other
six commissioners were trying Sir Robert Ker's invasion.
The other bills were divided,—Sir Robert Cary, two deputy
wardens and assizers of both nations with two of the
commissioners taking robberies and six of the commissioners deciding cases of murder.[75] They began with the
latest offence according to border custom and law,[76] which
as a recent writer points out was at least one of the reasons for so much difficulty in securing redress for offences.[77] On account of the comparatively short time allowed for the proving of so many complaints both at
days of truce, and at meetings of commissioners, the grievances of long standing, would seldom be reached, and even
if they were, there was a constantly increasing probability
of the death or disappearance of principals and witnesses.
All who were complained of and who did not appear at the
day of truce were to be filed absolutely. A grand jury
was empannelled to investigate cases.[78] As a result of
their sessions there was a total of 376 English bills and
204 Scotch bills filed.[79] The balance was to be settled at
appointed days of truce at the border.[80] The commission
ers agreed on the entry of pledges for the bills filed as
follows: Two or more of every broken clan were to be
entered. The warden himself was to enter a gentleman
for those not of any known clan. When entered they were
to be kept by indifferent men, not offended parties.
Pledges were to remain until the bills were satisfied; if
any should die, another was to take his place; and, finally,
if the bills were not satisfied within a year the hostage

---

[75] C. B. P., II, 494.
[76] Ibid, 486.
[77] "The Wardens of the Northern Marches," p. 24.
[78] C. B. P., II, 481, 550.
[79] Ibid, 520, 607, 608. These numbers are for the East and West
Marches only.
[80] Ibid, 560.

might be executed and another might be demanded.[81] This last provision does not seem to have been carried out.[82]

On finishing the work the commissioners caused proclamation to be made at the market crosses of the head boroughs of the marches in both realms, forbidding the inhabitants thereof to disturb the peace.[83]

In spite of the power of the commissioners we find evidence that their work was often badly done. The leaving of many bills to be filed by the wardens, to whom were also turned over the arrangements for the delivery of offenders, the non-sustaining of Lord Scrope in his refusal to submit his rolls to the commissioners till he was assured of the punishment of Buccleugh for the rescue of Kinmont Willie,[84]—all point to a hesitation on the part of Elizabeth and her ministers to do anything which might seriously endanger her peaceful relations with Scotland. The commission had hardly finished its work when Lord Willoughby complained that the bills filed were not sworn, that innocent were delivered for guilty and that the wardens could not remedy the commissioners' omissions.[85] Affairs seem no better than in 1559, when the Earl of Northumberland complained to Sadler that the Earl of Bothwell denied responsibility for the carrying out of pledges made by the commissioners.[86]

It does not appear that the commissions ever secured a complete clearing of the docket, but at least one more step was made toward full justice. The lack of decision and force on the part of both commissioners and wardens in dealing with Scotch matters is in striking contrast to the vigor of border administration when only English offenders were involved.

[81] Ibid, 594.
[82] C. B. P., II, 1166.
[83] Ibid, 621.
[84] Ibid, 491, 497, 506.
[85] Ibid, 1137.
[86] C. S. P., For., 1559-1560, 75.

CHAPTER VI

Just as the days of truce were the ordinary means of enforcing the provisions of the treaties, so the warden courts enforced the statutes and customs of the borders that applied to disturbances by Englishmen over whom the warden had jurisdiction, and to offences by Scots that were pursued by trod and taken red-handed.[1] Warden courts were generally kept at some place in the march for which the court was held,[2] but this custom was not invariable.[3]

These courts were in form and procedure very much like an ordinary court of oyer and terminer and gaol-delivery, with the exception that they exercised a more summary or martial power.

When the warden decided that the holding of a court was desirable for the peace of his march, he directed his warden-serjeant to warn the country and to proclaim that a court would be held on such a day appointed and that all who had complaints were to send in the names of the offenders to the warden or to the officer of a certain district, within, for example, ten days.[4] The warden, gentlemen, and country assembled at the appointed place and went to the Moot Hall, whereupon the warden-serjeant commanded that all should keep silence and hear the queen's commission of wardenry read. This done, the serjeant returned his panel of those who had been sum-

---

[1] Warden Court is sometimes used as a name for the meeting at a day of truce. It should be used only for the courts martial held by wardens for the trial of march treason.

[2] C. B. P., I, 835.

[3] Ibid, 507.

[4] C. S. P., For., 1569-1570, 768.

moned, and their names were called one after another
until enough were secured to serve as a grand jury. The
foreman, and then the rest of the jury were sworn to make
true presentment and inquiry of all things that should be
given into their charge. The charge was then read to the
jury, covering the list of crimes known as march treasons.

All men were then commanded to bring in any complaints or bills concerning matters triable in a warden
court. Recognizances and sureties were then to be called
if there were any. The grand jury then deliberated on
their verdict. When the bills were brought in, the prisoners were brought to the bar, one after another, and
arraigned for march treason and each was asked whether
or not he was guilty. If he said he was not guilty, the
trial went on with a trial jury of gentlemen, the prisoners
having leave to challenge. After such a jury was secured,
its members were sworn to make a true deliverance between the prisoner and the Queen. The prisoner was then
arraigned for a second time before the trial jury and
asked if he had anything to say for himself. The prisoner
having been heard, the jury was charged to inquire and
find whether A. B. prisoner at the bar was guilty of the
march treason of which he was indicted and arraigned
and whether he fled upon committing the act. If he was
found guilty, inquiry was also to be made as to what
lands, goods and tenements he had when the crime was
committed and of what value they were. The witnesses
were then called for, and after hearing them, the jury
went apart to agree upon a verdict. In giving their verdict the jury was to be polled, each one announcing
'guilty' or 'not guilty.' After the judgment was pro-
nounced by the Lord Warden in all the cases, the court
was adjourned till a new proclamation was made that another court was to be held.[5]

[5] State Papers, Borders, XLI, 1543. The order of procedure in

It is easily seen that there was no radical difference in procedure between the warden and other courts. The oaths of the jurors were almost word for word the same as are to-day used in the courts of oyer and terminer. The prisoner does not appear to have been represented by counsel or attorney. It, however, seems to have been difficult even for the warden to obtain a lawyer in the borders, and in any event the rights of accused persons have only comparatively recently been so safeguarded in our ordinary courts.

The principal difference was in the matters included in the charge to the jury of indictment. Many of the offences can easily be identified as having been included under one or another of the statutes, such as the selling of horses into Scotland and the taking or giving of blackmail. In other cases, however, the statutory basis for punishment is not so clear.

The offences may be grouped into three classes,—first, offences which directly or indirectly in peace or war brought danger or hurt to England or Englishmen through traffic of any sort with the Scotch; second, offences in which English dealt with English but in which Scotland or the Scotch were involved in any way; third, offences which involve danger or disturbance to Scotland or Scotchmen by English during time of peace. Thirty-one different offences are named in the state papers. It was march treason to persuade or bring any Scotchman into England in order to slaughter, burn or steal; to accompany him during the commission of any of these offences, or to give him aid or comfort afterwards; to furnish any arms or munitions of war of any sort, or any provisions

a warden court is given in great detail in this document. A similar manuscript from a private library giving the same details is quoted in Nicholson's "History of Westmorland and Cumberland," Introduction, p. XXIII. A number of verbal variations indicate that neither document is copied from the other.

of corn, leather, wool, felt, iron, etc., or any horses or nags, either to a Scot or to an Englishman to be sold to a Scot, without the special license of the Lord Warden in writing.

It was also march treason for an Englishman to give information to Scots in time of war, to marry a Scot, to take timber into Scotland or gold or silver above the value of 40s. at a time; or for an Englishman not to join the fray against the Scotch either when the offence was of his own knowledge or when called upon by the warden or by the searchers or watchers; to agree with a Scot to commit any rebellion in England; to liberate, without the license of the Lord Warden, a Scot taken red-handed; or, to join with a Scot in counterfeiting English or foreign coin.

The second group of offences concerns dealings of English with English which would bring injury to other Englishmen. It was, for example, march treason for an Englishman to convey an English offender into Scotland or to help him in any way, or to file a Scotch bill wrongfully on an Englishman; to hinder an Englishman from following trod, or to interfere in any way with the authorities, or to neglect to keep watches as well against English thieves as against the Scotch; or, to be disobedient in any other respect, or to take or give blackmail either from or to a Scot or another Englishman.

Finally, there is a third group of offences which governed the behavior of the English toward the realm of Scotland and its inhabitants in time of peace. It was march treason, therefore, to raise any rebellion in Scotland, to receive a Scotch rebel, to take prisoner a Scot who was traveling in England with the license of the Lord Warden, or to seize and detain his goods, or to rob a Scotchman residing in England with license, or to call wrongfully for the entering of any Scotchman at a day of truce.

The close relationship of the office of warden with the ordinary administration of justice is indicated by the fact

that the warden of the Middle March was *custos rotulorum*
for the county of Northumberland and the warden of the
West March *custos rotulorum* for Cumberland. The office
in Westmorland was held by a gentleman of that county
in 1584,[6] and we have no record of its having ever been
held by the warden.

The people tried in these courts were English "traitors"
and Scots who were taken red-handed in England or in
Scotland after fresh pursuit.[7] The English who caused
most of the trouble were dwellers along the Rede and
Tyne and were notorious throughout England for their
outlawry and ill-behavior. Harrison says of them: "In
this countrie also are the three vales or dales whereof men
haue doubted whether theeves or true men doo most
abound in them, that is to saie, Riddesdale, Tindale and
Liddesdale" and continues by saying that through the
good efforts of Master Gilpin and other ministers of the
gospel their "former sauage demeanor is verie much
abated."[8] The Society of Merchant Adventurers of
Newcastle-upon-Tyne ordained in 1554, "That no fre
brother of this Fellysshype shall from hensfourthe take
non apprentice to serve in this Fellysshype of non suche as
is or shalbe borne or brought up in Tyndall, Ryddisdall
or anye suche lycke places; in payne of XX£" and to
this was added "whereas the parties there brought upp
ar knowen either by educatyon or nature, not to be of
honest conversation."[9]

When any of the dwellers within a march committed
march treason it was the business of the warden serjeant

6 Collection of Ordinances for the Royal Household, etc., p. 274;
C. B. P., II, 184, 862.
7 Ibid, 1522.
8 Harrison's "Description of England," in Holinshed's Chronicles,
I, p. 154. Ed. London, 1807.
9 "Merchant Adventures of Newcastle-upon-Tyne," Surtees Soc.
Pub., XCIII, pp. 27, 28.

to arrest them, as he was the constable of the warden court.[10] The warden, however, might call on the sheriffs of all the northern counties for assistance.[11]

Most march treasons were felonies by statute and some of them were without benefit of clergy. Others again were punished by fines or imprisonment and in some instances by the assessment of damages upon the offender to be paid to the party grieved.

The death penalty for march treason was usually inflicted by beheading. For example, Sir John Forster held a warden court at Morpeth in 1567, and tried thirteen people, whereof six were beheaded,[12] and in 1587, Lord Hunsdon wrote to Burghley to tell him that much of the riding and spoiling in the Middle March was due to the neglect of Mr. Ridley and Mr. Heron and that he suspects Mr. Ridley and some other Englishmen of bringing in Scots, "whiche," he says, "if I find trewe, I will make them hopp heddles."[13] The next year Lord Hunsdon brought Ridley and Heron before a warden court at Alnwick where they refused to stand trial but submitted themselves to her majesty's mercy. It does not appear whether they were eventually pardoned or executed.[14] Sometimes, however, traitors were hanged instead of being beheaded.[15]

In 1595, Lord Eure wrote to Burghley that he was hunting out English felons and march traitors and was going to hold a court to reform them. Shortly afterwards he wrote that he intended holding a warden court the next day after a session of oyer and terminer and gaol delivery, because as it touched life and death, he wanted the

10 Cott. Ms. Calig., B. VIII, f. 405.
11 C. S. P., Dom., Add., 1580-1625, Eliz. XXXII, 59.
12 C. S. P., For., 1566-1568, 917.
13 C. B. P., I, 463.
14 Ibid, 601.
15 Cary's Memoirs, pp. 69-70; State Papers, Borders, XLI, f. 62.

assistance of the gravest in the north.[16] This seems clearly
to indicate a difference between the administration of civil
and military justice.

When Scotch thieves were taken they were hanged, although the right to do this was challenged on occasion by
the Scotch King who claimed that such a right belonged
only to the Scotch warden.[17] In 1595, Robert Cary sent
out part of the garrison of Berwick to watch for some
Scotch thieves. When the latter were caught, "They were
no sooner brought before me but a jury went upon them
and being found guilty they were presently hanged."[18]
In 1564, at York, out of thirteen border thieves who were
arraigned, seven were executed; and at Newcastle, of fourteen condemned, thirteen were executed.[19] On another occasion Cary again speaks of executing a thief.[20] In 1600,
Lord Scrope wrote to Cecil that they had just executed
three Scotch thieves, among them an Ellot, "in whose be-
halfe the King sent to mee very earnestly, but I had no
laysure at the tyme and so the thief was hanged before I
knew the King's pleasure."[21] And in 1587, Lord Hunsdon at a court held at Alnwick for the West and Middle
Marches, executed a number of thieves, both English and
Scotch.[22]

In the case of minor offences the punishment was ordi-
narily fixed by statute. Sometimes the offence was agreed
upon by the warden and the gentlemen of his wardenry
as one to be punished as a dangerous practice. This
was the case when Lord Scrope took up the question

[16] C. B. P., II, 187, 188, 227.
[17] State Papers, Borders, XLI, f. 162; C. B. P., II, 1492, 1495,
1508.
[18] Cary's Memoirs, pp. 69-70.
[19] C. S. P., Dom., Add., 1547-1565, Eliz. XII, 21.
[20] C. B. P., II, 373, 374.
[21] Ibid, 1264.
[22] C. B. P., I, 507.

of blackmail in the West March. It was to be punished
by six months' imprisonment and, in addition, the offender
was to be fined £5 sterling. Later, a statute made the
giving or taking of blackmail punishable by death.[23]

If the offenders could not be captured, their homes and
barns were burned by order of the warden and they were
proclaimed outlaws.[24]

Just as there was trouble in securing redress at a day
of truce so there was difficulty in the punishment of
march treason in a warden court.

In the first place there was some dispute as to what constituted march treason. A memorandum of 1590, gives as
undisputed march treasons the carrying of horses into
Scotland, conveying arms or weapons or munitions into
Scotland, betraying the persons or goods of Englishmen,
and wilfully suffering Scotch murderers to escape. Disputed march treasons were to tryst or hold converse with
a Scot without the license of the warden, to tryst with a
Scot with license of the warden but about matters of
march treason, or to travel in Scotland without a license
from the warden. It was, however, not march treason to
make a raid into Scotland by day or night to steal or rob.[25]
But even if this dispute had been settled, there remained
other difficulties which interfered with the efficiency of
the warden courts.

The appeal of important Scotch persons to delay the enforcement of the law has been already mentioned.[26] In
addition, there was always the question of compounding
felonies. English law is strict with respect to this practice but there are many examples of it on the borders,[27]

[23] Nicholson's "Leges Marchiarum," pp. 113, etc.
[24] C. B. P., II, 1479.
[25] Cott. Ms. Calig., B. VIII, ff. 401, 402.
[26] C. B. P., II, 1479.
[27] C. S. P., Dom., Add., 1566-1579, entries for 1570, passim.
Rebels compound for escheats, etc.

particularly where relations with Scotland were involved. For example, Lord Scrope wrote in 1594, that he had taken two English thieves in Scotland and that he had received such offers for their release as were never before made.[28]

Other circumstances interfering with the enforcement of the law were the constant appeals of victims that the lives of those who had injured them should be spared, since they were afraid of entering into a feud. For instance, Sir Cuthbert Collingwood wrote in 1587, saying that John Hand of Atterbury and all his friends petition that certain thieves (Trumbulls, Douglasses and others) should be spared, for if they were executed, according to their deserts, it would be an everlasting trouble to the said John Hand.[29]

Somewhat allied to this was the difficulty of getting convictions owing to intermarriages and friendships. For example, Lord Eure held a warden court in 1596, at which there were about seventy prisoners but only three convictions. Some were so befriended that the jury sat that day and night and the next day and at night there was still no verdict. Lord Eure further wrote that he had for the safety of the gentlemen, withdrawn the prisoner by the advice of her majesty's counsel, though not agreeable to common law. The jury rested without meat or drink, according to border custom.[30] Still another complaint arose from the existence of independent jurisdictions within the wardenry. The officers of these districts made private arrangements with English and Scotch offenders without the knowledge of the warden.[31] This was march treason as well as interference with justice but does not

28 C. B. P., I, 980.
29 State Papers, Borders, XXV, f. 173.
30 C. B. P., II, 249.
31 C. B. P., I, 662.

seem ever to have been punished. Finally, there were
two or three provisions of the laws which were never seriously enforced. One of these forbade the selling of horses
into Scotland, about which we find constant complaints
but which seemed still to continue almost unabated until
the end of Elizabeth's reign. The others related to the
presence of Scotch persons in the marches and Berwick,
and to intermarriages of English with Scotch. These provisions were practically never enforced in the later years.[32]
In 1563, the Queen gave special permission to a Scotch
minister to serve the town of Berwick,[33] and in 1574, the
customer of Berwick was proven to be a Scot. He lost his
office and was apparently banished.[34] In February, 1568,
there were four hundred forty-three Scots residing in the
East March in defiance of border law [35] and there is constant complaint of the presence of the Scotch in the suggestions for improvements of border affairs.[36] One John
Anell complained in June, 1586, to Mr. Randolph, one of
Elizabeth's commissioners for the borders, that he had
been put off his tenancy in the Middle March and a
Scotsman installed in it, and that since Candlemas four
other Scotch families had been brought in. Randolph says
in a note that this custom was so common that an Englishman could not get nor keep any land; that Menelaws (a
district in the Middle March) had not an Englishman in
it; and that every third man within ten miles of the border in the East and Middle Marches is a Scot.[37]

The border lords not only granted tenantries to Scots
but often employed them as retainers and servants. For
example, Launcelot Carleton complained that Thomas Mus-

[32] C. B. P., I, 75, 435, 834; C. B. P., II, 213, 1192, etc.
[33] C. S. P., For., 1563, 1138.
[34] Ibid, 1572-1574, 1327, 1383, 1392.
[35] Ibid, 1566-1568, 2015, 2133.
[36] Ibid; C. B. P., I, 165, 834.
[37] C. B. P., I, 435.

grave had made Bewcastle a den of thieves and a harbor of murderers and felons, Scotch and English.[38] Besides these reasons frequent intermarriages not only brought Scots into England but probably also prevented the enforcement of the full penalty of the law. Lord Eure, in 1596, suggested that instead of imprisoning them and confiscating their goods that it might disturb their King less to quietly put them and their goods over the boundary.[39]

On the whole, however, march law appears to have been administered with promptness and severity. The only evidence of miscarriage of justice is that given by Lord Eure and we learn elsewhere that he had not the confidence of his subordinates and eventually either resigned under charges or was removed from office. Lord Hunsdon did not have any trouble in securing a large percentage of convictions in 1587, while he was warden of the Middle March during the suspension of Sir John Forster.

[38] C. B. P., II, 1361.
[39] Ibid, 213.

CHAPTER VII

THE DEFENCE OF THE BORDERS

In addition to the enforcement of penalties for disorders and other crimes by means of the trials at days of truce and in warden courts, the peace and safety of the borders were secured through a system of defence maintained chiefly to protect the marches from incursions by the Scotch.

According to the custom on the borders as well as by the provisions of their leases, holders of castles or towers were required to maintain them in proper condition for defence, and their sub-tenants were bound in turn to maintain horse and armor for themselves, or else these had to be furnished by the lease holder.[1] In order to be certain of the condition of the mounts and armor, musters were held regularly twice each year in the marches.[2] A great part of the state papers is composed of lists of the men who appeared at the musters, coupled with a statement as to whether or not they had a horse, and the description of the armor with which they were provided. If the men themselves were not freeholders, it was stated also which lord was responsible for their being properly furnished.[3]

In the statements given of the results of the musters there appear great discrepancies from time to time. These differences do not seem to be always the result of neglect

[1] 2 and 3, Philip and Mary, Chapter I; C. B. P., I, 78, 159;. C. B. P., II, 268.

[2] The dates on which the musters were taken were about the 1st of April and of November.

[3] C. B. P., I and II, passim.

91

of the landlords properly to furnish their tenants, but may
be ascribed either to a different method of accounting or to
a difference in the care with which the musters were in-
spected. For example, a muster of the East March dated
March 10, 1579,[4] gives 323 horsed and furnished and 825
unfurnished, a total of 1,148. Another statement dated
March 31, of the same year, gives 363 furnished and 753
unfurnished. In the Middle March at the same time there
were 1,145 furnished and 525 unfurnished. In the West
March the muster masters found 520 furnished without
any mention of those who were not furnished. The next
year, Lord Scrope gives the number furnished only with
armor, etc., in the West March as 4,031, furnished with
nags, 679; unfurnished, 3,301, a total of 8,011.[5] Three
years later, in 1583, the total number of footmen in the
three marches is given as 15,133 of which 7,174 were furnished with armor and 7,959 unfurnished.[6] The improvement in administration in the latter part of Elizabeth's
reign must have brought about an increase of population
on the borders, for in 1593, the whole number mustered
on the borders is given as 7,298 horse and 13,348 foot, a
total of 20,646 able men,[7] which would indicate a population of about one hundred thousand. Lord Scrope's clerk
gives, in an estimate made about 1585, a total of 15,072
able men in the West Wardenry alone. This probably included all men between the ages of sixteen and sixty.
These were the border militia and were all bound to serve
when called upon by the Lord Lieutenant or by the warden.[8] But Willoughby says in 1600, that Scrope had ten

[4] This date should probably be 1580, as it is joined with the two
following of that year.
[5] Bowes' Collection of Border Causes, Nos. 8, 9, 10, 12 in State
Papers, Borders, XX, 76; C. B. P., I, 47, 48, 54, 94.
[6] C. B. P., I, 160.
[7] C. S. P., Dom., Add., 1580-1625, Eliz. XXXII, 77.
[8] "Nicholson's History of Westmorland and Cumberland," Intro.,
p. LXXXIX; A. P. C., 1587, March 29 and Nov. 1.

or twelve thousand able men,[9] and this under circumstances where Willoughby would have stated the largest
possible number. It seems impossible to reconcile this difference. It is also hard to account for the sudden shrink-
age between 1593 and 1595 that is indicated in the musters taken in Northumberland, in those years. These give
a total of 920 light horse in 1593 and of only 136 in 1595.[10]
It is just possible that the continued peace with Scotland
and better control by the wardens had made it safer as
well as more profitable to raise cattle instead of horses,
for as far back as 1559, the musters indicate 1,830 horse
and 2,988 footmen, a very creditable showing as compared
with the later years.[11]

The Bishop of Durham was liable for border service from the County Palatine. In 1596, he claimed the
privilege of serving with his levies on the borders for only
fourteen days on their own charges and then to take the
queen's pay if they served longer.[12] They were bound to
come only on the call of the Warden of the East or of the
West March; if it was to resist invasion the usual muster
from the Bishopric was one thousand, but only five hundred if they were to be employed in Scotland. The warden assembled the Bishopric by writing to the Bishop if
the latter was in the county, if not, to the sheriff and the
other officers.[13]

Westmorland seems not to have been much depended
on for border service on account of its distance from Scotland and the lack of familiarity of its inhabitants with
border stratagem.[14]

The border lords, their servants and tenants were called
together for service either by the burning of beacons by

9 C. B. P., II, 1193.
10 Ibid, 168, 169, 170, 173, 174.
11 C. S. P., For., 1558-1559, 365.
12 C. B. P., II, 234.
13 State Papers, Borders, XX, 76.
14 C. B. P., II, 1435.

night, by proclamations in market towns, or by letters
sent to the gentlemen, officers and chief men within the
district, appointing the time and place of assembly.[15] How
this militia was used after it was assembled appears in
many places in the state papers. For example, the troops
were required to attend the warden several times each
year into Scotland for two nights and one day going and
coming, for the purpose of holding a day of truce. Often
they were called for more serious work. On one occasion
Lord Scrope placed five hundred men in blue coats at Kers-
hopefoot to ward off attacks from Scotland.[16] At another
he called together five or six hundred borderers at Carlisle
to keep the Scotch wardens, Lords Morton, Herries and
their attendants, home from Edinburgh, and promised
to repeat his action if the king should again summon the
Scots against the assembly of nobles at St. Johnstons.[17]
On still another occasion Richard Lowther, the deputy
warden of the West March went to the boundary with one
thousand men on account of trouble between Bothwell
and the King of Scots. Just after the execution of Queen
Mary, Sir John Forster warned all the gentlemen in his
wardenry to provide armor and weapons and be ready
with their tenants to repel any sudden invasion from
Scotland,[18] and again in 1593, he issued a similar order
to be read in the parish churches.[19] In 1601, Sir Robert
Cary wrote to Cecil and told him that sixty of the gentlemen and their followers had come to the wastes and
stayed five weeks at "The Fort in the Heynyng."[20]

In addition to the maintenance of the border militia,
the towns and parishes along the border were bound to

[15] State Papers, Borders, XX, 76.
[16] C. B. P., I, 196.
[17] C. B. P., I, 212.
[18] Ibid, 491.
[19] Ibid, 901.
[20] C. B. P., II, 1400.

maintain watches, beacons and slew dogs. The orders for the watches made in 1555, by Lord Wharton, Lord Warden General of the Marches, appear to have been the basis for the arrangement which continued during the reign of Elizabeth.[21] Sussex, the Lieutenant General of the North, Lord Scrope, and Sir John Forster renewed and increased them in 1570, and Lord Scrope again reestablished them in 1593. Unfortunately, there are not many details in the records of the intervening years. It appears, however, that the watches were laid spasmodically as danger threatened rather than regularly placed. The fact that the watches had to be furnished and paid by the county[22] may have been the reason of this laxness in administration. Lord Scrope at one time writing to Burghley, spoke of being compelled to keep one hundred county men on watch for a fortnight, and in another letter, said that he had laid a plump watch[23] of forty horse every night, which the county would be unable to stand for any time.[24] Lord Eure in 1597, ordered a plump watch of forty men to be kept in Morpeth Ward (in the Middle March) and the same year Cary informed Burghley that the Scots had come as far as Alnwick and had taken the watches.[25] In 1601, there is record that there was "such watching in Penrith on the night as was not one hundred years before. Fifty watchers nightly."[26]

Watches and beacons are usually mentioned together in the provisions for defence. The latter was one of the

[21] C. S. P., For., 1569-1571, 1392; C. B. P., I, 834; Nicholson's "Leges Marchiarum," Appendix, pp. 209-323.

[22] C. S. P., For., 1558-1559, 169; 1560-1561, 735; C. B. P., II, 458; Burghley Papers, Haynes, I, pp. 217-220.

[23] "Plump watch" was composed of a group of horse or foot instead of single watchers.

[24] C. B. P., II, 114, 458.

[25] Ibid, 351, 831.

[26] "Town records of Carlisle" quoted in "Northumberland and the Borders"; by Walter White, London, 1859.

methods for calling the borderers to arms and was also the
usual method of giving warning of the approach of Scotch
raiders.[27] Lord Wharton's orders in 1555 gave a list of
twenty places in the West March where provisions for
beacon fires were to be maintained,[28] and as late as 1596
they were still used for their customary purposes.[29]

One of the most curious points in connection with the
defence of the borders is the keeping of what were called
slew dogs or sleuth hounds. These dogs were, like the
watches and beacons, to be maintained by the county or
by the various towns, and were evidently used for the
tracking of offenders to their homes. In 1596, Lord Eure
ordered that they should be kept in convenient places and
money levied, or an allowance made to maintain them, on
pain of fine and imprisonment *ex antiquo*.[30] Some of the
dwellers on the marches kept such dogs for their own satisfaction and to serve the county, which the county would
not have been able to pay for.[31] Edward Grey, who served
as deputy warden of the Middle March during the trial of
Lord Eure, asked for a "Kallendar" by which he could
call the dogs in their several divisions,[32] and, finally, we
find that the men belonging to the garrison at Hexham
who lived more than five miles away kept slew dogs.[33]
Some of them were of considerable value. For example,
among a list of fifty-eight bills filed between the Middle
March of England and the Keepership of Liddesdale in
Scotland in 1590, there is one which claimed that the
Scots had stolen several horses valued at from twenty

[27] C. B. P., I, 783; C. S. P., Dom., Add., 1566-1579, Eliz. XVII,
101, 102, 107, 108.
[28] Nicholson's "History of Westmorland and Cumberland," Intro.,
p. XLIV; C. B. P., II, 336; C. B. P., I, 783.
[29] C. B. P., II, 336.
[30] C. B. P., II, 536; Hist. Mss. Com., 3rd Report, App., p. 39.
[31] C. B. P., II, 652.
[32] Ibid, 831.
[33] Ibid, 854.

shillings to five pounds, a sword and spear worth twenty
shillings and a slew dog worth ten pounds.[34] In the
whole fifty-eight bills there is no horse worth so much.
Evidently these hounds were an important part of the
system of border defence.

In addition to this general border service, the garrisons
maintained by the crown at various towns and castles
were, with considerable frequency, drawn upon by the
wardens for the defence of the borders. The chief of these
towns was Berwick, which, although not within the bounds
of any march, was considered as part of the borders. The
governor of Berwick was almost invariably warden of the
East March and consequently used his garrison in enforcing the laws of the marches within his jurisdiction. The
number of men at Berwick varied from time to time but
the smallest number seems to be that reported by Lord
Hunsdon in 1569. In a letter to the Privy Council, he
wrote that the garrison of Berwick was five hundred,
many old and hurt in service and more suitable for an
almshouse than to be soldiers.[35] In 1559, however, the
garrison had been 2,190 men,[36] which was shortly reduced
to 1,850,[37] and by 1564, the number of men was still
further reduced to a few more than nine hundred. This
number appears to have remained as the usual garrison of
Berwick during the rest of the reign of Elizabeth.[38]

In the "Establishment for Berwick" made by Elizabeth
in 1560, we find some curious provisions regarding the soldiers there. They had to wear jackets of the queen's colors,
white and green, and were not to wear any other livery

[34] C. B. P., I, 668. Even under James the slew dogs were kept
by the county to track criminals. Nicholson's "History of Westmorland and Cumberland," Intro., p. CXXXI.
[35] C. S. P., For., 1569-1571, 568.
[36] Ibid, 1559-1560, 402.
[37] Sadler State Papers, Vol. II, p. 7.
[38] C. S. P., For., 1564-1565, 185; C. B. P., I, 537, etc.

or cognizance save the queen's. They were not to use any
vile occupation such as fishing; they were not to use dice
or cards for money, except within twenty days of Christ-
mas, nor to play dice at night except they were of the
Council,[39] etc.

Holy and Farne Islands were garrisoned by a captain
from the garrison of Berwick with one hundred men. The
captain of Tynemouth had a retinue of sixteen gunners
and servants paid by the queen. The gunner and constable
of Norham were paid by the queen while the rest of the
garrison, like the garrisons of Alnwick and Harbottle, was
maintained by those who held this place from the crown.
Carlisle had a total garrison, including gunners, porters,
watchers, etc., of thirty-six in the queen's pay. The Captain of Bewcastle and the Land-serjeant of Gilsland each
maintained a retinue out of their fees. In time of serious
trouble or danger on the marches, the Privy Council,
either on its own initiative or in response to appeals from
the wardens sent troops to the borders from other northern counties, or else loaned troops from Berwick to the
Middle or West Marches. For example, in 1559, before
peace with Scotland was finally settled, the Privy Council
sent word to the Earl of Northumberland that one thousand men were to be levied from the borders, five hundred
from the Bishopric of Durham, two hundred from the
North Riding of York and three hundred from Richmond-
shire,[40] and later in the year another levy of seven hundred was made in Staffordshire, Warwickshire and Shrop-
shire[41] on account of the activity of the French in Scotland. In 1568, one hundred horse were levied in Durham
for the Middle March.[42] In 1569, on account of the Rising

[39] C. S. P., For., 1560-1561, 514.
[40] C. S. P., For., 1558-1559, 230, 483.
[41] Ibid, 1373.
[42] C. S. P., Dom., Add., 1566-1579, Eliz. XIV, 19.

in the North there were sudden and extensive levies of troops made.[43] During the ten years from 1570 to 1580, the ordinary defences of the borders seemed to prove sufficient for there are few hints of special levies of troops. In 1573, Elizabeth sent extra troops to the borders to help the Scotch king in his troubles with the Catholic party.[44] In 1581, the Earl of Huntingdon sent twenty-five hundred troops to the borders for the assistance of Her Majesty's party in Scotland.[45] On this occasion, Robert Bowes complained bitterly about Elizabeth's parsimony in connection with her relations with Scotland, saying that money spent promptly would save ten times as much spent to protect the borders later on.[46] The same year, the Privy Council instructed Huntingdon to put fifty shot from Berwick at Harbottle and to supply their places with men from Yorkshire.[47]

In 1583, Lord Scrope wrote to Walsingham to refute the charge that the troops from Berwick had been but of little service, stating that they were always able with these foot to do three or four ill turns for one.[48] This detail from Berwick to Carlisle was repeated for at least the two following years, and in 1585, Sir John Forster also received warrants to support an extra garrison at Harbottle Castle in the Middle March.[49] Again in 1587, Davison informed Lord Scrope that the queen had permitted the latter to levy fifty horse against any sudden incursion and enclosed warrants for their pay.[50] The necessity for this

[43] C. S. P., For., 1569-1571, 508, 613, 616, 686, etc.; Sadler State Papers, Vol. II, passim.
[44] C. S. P., For., 1572-1574, 1076.
[45] Correspondence of Robert Bowes, Sur. Soc. Pub., Vol. XIV, pp. 165-166.
[46] Ibid, 252, 263, 283, 296, etc.
[47] C. B. P., I, 519.
[48] Ibid, 158, 182.
[49] Ibid, 219, 270, 306, 320, 373, etc.
[50] Ibid, 480.

precaution was the execution of the Queen of Scots. At
the same time one hundred fifty horse and one hundred
foot were granted for the Middle March and five hundred
lay on the borders under command of Lord Hunsdon,
warden of the East March.[51]

In May, 1592, Christopher Dacre suggested that the
queen and the West March should together support a garrison of one hundred men for six months.[52]   In 1593,
Scrope again asked for forty or fifty horse [53] and in 1596-
1597, Lord Eure received warrants from time to time for
the maintenance of eighty horse in the Middle March for
a year.[54]   Lord Willoughby in 1600, protested against
troops from Berwick being sent to the West March, where,
he said, Lord Scrope had ten or twelve thousand able men
with but little opposite.[55]

Elizabeth frequently refused the troops asked for, upon
which wardens sometimes devised schemes by which extra
troops could be maintained at little expense to the crown.
Lord Scrope's plan to use money raised for distressed soldiers and mariners for the support of a garrison in
Brough for Henry Leigh has already been mentioned. A
little later, in 1595, Scrope begged the Privy Council to
send a letter to the gentlemen of the county to levy such
sums amongst them as would support Sir Henry Leigh
and so avoid the necessity of going to the frontier themselves.[56]   A similar proposal of a tax for the purpose of
supporting garrisons at several places is found in a note
to Burghley written in 1576.[57]   On another occasion Lord
Eure proposed that if the queen would furnish and pay

[51] Ibid, 486, 564.
[52] Ibid, 746.
[53] Ibid, 853.
[54] C. B. P., II, 397.
[55] Ibid, 1193.
[56] Ibid, 10.
[57] Ibid, 323.

for two hundred horsemen for five years, the gentlemen of his wardenry would furnish them with horses and armor out of their common funds, and besides they themselves would furnish another hundred complete. By this arrangement the queen would pay less than one-half the total cost, but it does not appear that she accepted the offer.[58]

Richard Lowther, as deputy warden of the West March, in 1601, proposed that the men of his wardenry should either furnish for its defence one hundred horse chosen by themselves or fifty horse chosen by the warden. They refused to do either, but offered fifty horse to be chosen by themselves. Lowther wrote to Cecil asking that the Council commend them to the justices of the peace and the worshipful of the county,[59] apparently with the object of having them punished in some way.

The townsmen of Carlisle were willing to render their share of border service though legally they did not have to do so. Lord Scrope asked that they be permitted to purchase some armor from the queen's stores for which they would pay part and Scrope would take bonds for the balance or re-deliver the munitions. Not long afterward the tenants of Brough were granted a similar request.[60] Later on, Lord Scrope had some trouble in collecting the money and complained of the queen's high prices.[61] Lord Willoughby in 1600, made a similar request that the people of the East March be permitted to purchase condemned arms at reasonable rates.[62]

There is one record of troops levied in the marches for service elsewhere. On October 8, 1566, the Privy Council

[58] Ibid, 707.
[59] Ibid, 1356, 1359, 1362.
[60] Ibid, 258, 289.
[61] Ibid, 472.
[62] Ibid, 1152.

ordered that fifty horse for Ireland be levied in the West March and a like number in the East March.[63]

As we have already seen the statutes provided that the queen from time to time might appoint a commission whose business it was to see that the castles and towers within twenty miles of the borders were kept in proper condition for defence, that enclosures were made in order to check the invasions of the Scots by leaving the way of retreat less open, and in general to see to the better defence of that part of the kingdom. The first commission appears to have been granted by Elizabeth in 1561 to the Earl of Rutland and others.[64] Their report dated August, 1561, provided that enclosures or crofts of not more than two or less than one-half acre should be made of the lands adjoining each town or village along the boundary. These enclosures were to be surrounded by ditches four feet deep and six feet broad, set with double quicksett and with some ash trees. Inland fields were to be separated from each other with like ditches and hedges, but no enclosure was to exceed thirty acres. All commons were to be similarly ditched and hedged or walled with stone or surrounded by great trenches. The cost of this work was to be borne by the inheritor or tenant for life and was to be done as the surveyors should decide. Tenants for seven years were to sow hips and haws and shoots of ash trees at such places as the surveyors should prescribe. For the repair of castles, towers and houses of stone the owners should employ the fifth part of their yearly revenue.

The queen's castles and lands were to be surveyed and orders taken for their repair and enclosure. The surveyors were to certify yearly to the commissioners, before October first, how much each man was to ditch and enclose each year and before Easter how much had been

63 C. S. P., Dom., Add., 1566-1579, Eliz. XIII, 33.
64 C. S. P., For., 1561-1562, 370.

done and the default. Surveyors found negligent were to be reported to the queen and council and fined at the discretion of the commissioners.

In the East March the inhabitants within four miles of the Tweed were to make, near the fords of that river, a main ditch six feet deep and eight broad, and were to cut aslope the hills adjoining and make them so steep that no passage may be made by them. In the Middle March near Harbottle, there being many passes for horsemen, the people of Coquetdale were to enclose as much as was possible of their fields in a similar manner with walls of stone and by trenches. The wardens were to assist the surveyors, and every month or six weeks examine what was done and were to certify any defaults to the President of the North and the commissioners. Delinquent freeholders were to be fined. The surveyors were to provide carriage, wood, workmen, quicksett, etc., and were to pay according to the custom of Northumberland.[65]

The program laid down by the commissioners appears satisfactory enough, but about a year later, Lord Rutland wrote to Cecil saying that nothing had been done about enclosures, although for that year only 3,144 acres were to be enclosed, and that the state of the queen's lands was a bad example to the rest of the county.[66] The deliberation with which the provisions of the act were enforced was probably due to the opposition of the inhabitants of the marches, for in 1569, a mob of three hundred undertook to overthrow one of the enclosures so made.[67]

The energies of the government were apparently directed elsewhere for fifteen years or so, for the next definite piece of information is found in a note of 1580 by Sir

---

[65] Bowes' Collections of Border Causes No. 5 in State Papers, Borders, XX, 76; C. S. P., For., 1561-1562, 370.
[66] C. S. P., For., 1561-1562, 680.
[67] C. S. P., Dom., Add., 1566-1579, Eliz. XIV, 87.

John Forster, who speaks of a commission of survey having been appointed in 1563, at which very little was done. In January, 1581, there was an objection raised to a proposed bill for fortifying the borders, the plea being that its passage would make tenants discontented and that the devising of remedies might encourage complaints. However in the same year Henry, Earl of Huntingdon, and a long list of others were named as commissioners for border affairs.[68] The reports show many of the houses and castles decayed, among them Norham, Wark, Hexham and Naworth,[69] probably as a result of the rebellion of the northern earls in 1569-1570.

In 1583, three separate commissions were named, fourteen gentlemen being appointed to view the decays and defaults in the defences of the East March, and twelve each for similar purposes in the Middle and West Marches. There was the usual sequel of voluminous reports, but it does not appear that the improvement resulting from the work of these commissions was any greater than before.[70]

In 1585, Sir Robert Bowes was sent to view or survey the borders. Norham appears to have been repaired since 1581 as it is described in the survey as being well furnished. On the whole the condition of the forts and towers has not much improved. Bowes states as the cause of the decay that the owners withdrew to farms within the country where they could live more quietly, safely and cheaply than on the "uttermost border." The cost of a barnekin of timber is given as two hundred marks and to build a tower, one hundred pounds. Bowes thinks that some encouragement to build should be given through competent rewards, and that recompense be also given to owners whose forts have been destroyed by wars.[71]

68 C. B. P., I, 82, 83.
69 C. S. P., Dom., Add., 1580-1625, Eliz, XXVII, 44.
70 C. S. P., Dom., Add., 1580-1625, Eliz. XXVIII, 23, 25.
71 Bowes' Collections of Border Causes, No. 16, in State Papers, Borders, XX, 76.

In 1595, a general commission for investigating border
causes was given to Sir William Bowes, nephew of Robert
Bowes,[72] but in 1596, he mentions that he has been a commissioner for the last four years, which would date his
first commission in 1593.[73] There is no indication in the
records that much was done that would tend to bring
about a betterment of conditions, and there was certainly
not enough done to bring about a satisfactory solution of
the problem of protecting the English from the Scotch,
for as late as 1600, Lord Scrope wrote to the Privy Council suggesting measures for reform. Amongst them he
urged that a *legier* commission to be renewed yearly should
be issued to gentlemen of integrity to inquire and certify
decays and defaults to the warden.[74]

Running steadily through the whole reign of Elizabeth,
suggestions of various sorts are found amongst the state
papers which aim at improvements in the conduct of border affairs. These sometimes only point out the troubles,
leaving the remedies to be devised by others. In some
cases, however, there are recommendations which, if carried out, as they sometimes were, would bring about
an advance toward law and order. The first suggestion was offered in December, 1558, by the Earl of
Westmorland. He thought that the East and Middle
Marches should have separate wardens.[75] The Marquis
of Winchester in 1559, urged that Norham and Wark be
fortified, a suggestion that was adopted, and further that
the ground within ten miles of the border be divided into
five-mark holdings and the tenants compelled to provide
horse and armor, which was not adopted.[76] Lord Wharton

[72] C. B. P., II, 163.
[73] Ibid, 449, 814, 870; C. S. P., Dom., Add., 1580-1625, Eliz.
XXXII, 83.
[74] C. B. P., II, 1192.
[75] C. S. P., For., 1558-1559, 167. This idea was also suggested
by Sadler. Sadler State Papers, Vol. II, p. 13.
[76] C. S. P., For., 1558-1559, 1230.

recommended that the borders should have a governor of
great power, that the chief houses should be the queen's;
land should be granted for the support of officers; a council should be established, of whom two were to be learned
in the law; all offices should be held during the pleasure
of the queen instead of for life; that days of truce should
be held often; and warden courts at least twice a year; in-
heritors and officers should be resident, and that courts of
oyer and terminer were to be held at York, Newcastle and
Carlisle.[77] Sir John Forster said in 1561, that some tenants had absorbed the lands of others and that each tenant
should have no more land than he was accustomed to have.[78]
Again, in 1575, Forster wrote more extensively. He urged
as causes of decay the sale of horses into Scotland, and
leases held at second or third hand. The first taker pays
two or three years' fine and the sub-tenant ten years' fine
and so are utterly unable to keep horse or armor. Again,
when a man has a tenement big enough for one and has
two sons, he divides it between them.[79] This is elsewhere
in the state papers spoken of as a custom of the dales of
Tyne and Rede.[80] In 1580, Forster again has a list of
reasons for defaults, among which are "half-lands" or
divided inheritances; neglect of owners; small holdings,
excessive fines and "gressums,"[81] and raised rents, in
one case the rent was increased from forty shillings to five
pounds.[82] Another report of the same year complained
that castles and houses of defence were in the hands of non-
residents and that lands were let to Scots who could pay
higher rents than the English since their goods were not
stolen. The complaint further said that the land was not

[77] Ibid, 1560-1561, 551.
[78] Ibid, 1561-1562, 441.
[79] Ibid, 1575-1577, 167.
[80] Ibid, 268.
[81] A gressum was the sum paid for the renewal of a lease.
[82] C. B. P., I, 50.

planted and sowed, but given to sheep and so would not
support so many people and, finally, that the long peace
was yet another cause of the decay. Still another report
(of 1579) says that the indefinite power of the warden
and the uncertainty of march treason are the greatest
plagues of the borders since the wardens and borderers
never agree as to the cause of march treason.[83]

In 1587, there was a suggestion that the borders should
be fortified by means of "inskons" or "inskers," an
earthen redoubt or breastwork, which was to extend along
the northern boundary of England. If this was not possible it was suggested that the Roman wall be restored.[84]

Lord Thomas Scrope proposed in 1593 that the warden
should have fuller power to command arrests; that the
order for watches should be renewed and kept; that the
statute for hue and cry should be enforced; and that intermarriages with Scots should be forbidden. Suspected
persons were to be put in jail; Scots were not to be permitted to come into Westmorland or Cumberland above
Carlisle without the license of the warden.[85] Lord Eure, in
1595, suggested that the queen should remove all officers
connected with the Scots and put Yorkshire or inland gentlemen in their places,[86]—a proposition that would have
depleted his march of its gentry and which in all probability was the real cause of the charges which were
brought against him and which led to his resignation in
1598. The same year, 1595, the Master of Ordnance of
the North wrote to Burghley stating that though he was in
charge of the ordnance at Carlisle he had no control over
the gunners there and that when the places fell vacant,
the queen granted them for life to unsuitable and non-
resident men, and urged a change in the method of ap-

[83] C. B. P., I, 75; Cott. Ms. Calig., B. VIII, f. 400.
[84] Cott. Ms. Calig., C. II, f. 490; C. B. P., I, 581.
[85] Ibid, 834.
[86] C. B. P., II, 131.

pointment.[87] The next year Lord Eure suggested that as
the tenants were unable to provide horse and armor the
freeholders and copyholders of both the queen and subjects should bear that cost.[88] In 1598, Sir Robert Bowes
suggested the even division of Northumberland, from the
border to the Tyne, and thence to the sea. Over each division a deputy was to be placed and these were to divide
the fee of the Warden of the Middle March, the whole to
be under the charge of the Governor of Berwick assisted
by a council from the borders.[89] In 1600, Lord Scrope
formulated a new list of suggestions which included many
of the old ones. Foreign marriages were to be march
treason; Englishmen dwelling in Scotland were to return
by a certain date or be treated as traitors, and the Graemes
in the Debatable Lands were to be dealt with by statute
as they usurped royal jurisdiction and liberties.[90] Even
religion received some share of attention. In 1597, it was
proposed that part of the surplus of abbey lands, tithes
and unappropriated parsonages in Northumberland was
to be employed in maintaining preachers and three gram-
mar schools; all non-resident ministers and those who
could not preach, with benefices worth clearly forty pounds
a year were to be removed, and no recusant or any one
whose wife was a recusant was to have rule anywhere.[91]

Perhaps the most interesting suggestions are those proposing colonizing schemes. For instance, Lord Scrope suggested to Lord Burghley, in 1596, that the Graemes be deported to other parts of the kingdom and their places
filled with inland men.[92] This appears to be the result of
their aid to Buccleugh in the attack on Carlisle Castle and

87 C. B. P., II, 81.
88 Ibid, 268.
89 Ibid, 922.
90 Ibid, 192.
91 Ibid, 746.
92 Ibid, 253.

rescue of "Kinmont Willie" earlier in the year, and
seems to be the first mention of the plan which was later,
in 1606 and 1607, actually carried out by James.[93] The
same year (1596), Mr. Fern, who was captain of a company
at Berwick, proposed to Burghley that colonies should be
transferred to Tynedale from the other parts of the kingdom.[94] In 1597, Burghley made some notes to be considered by Bowes on his tour of inspection in the North.
Among other things the latter was to inquire how many
more were living on the borders than the natural soil
of the country could maintain; Burghley thought that it
might be necessary to have some multitude of the idle
people sent to other countries or to have them serve elsewhere; otherwise, Bowes was to consider if the multitude
living idle should not be forced to work and till the
ground.[95]

In many cases these suggestions made from time to time
by individuals became the policy of the government and
were carried out as well as possible in treaties, statutes,
instructions, and regulations by the commissioners, as has
already been seen. And while the provisions so laid down
were not always strictly enforced still there seems to have
been continuous efforts on the part of the authorities to
improve the administration of Berwick and the Marches.

[93] Muncaster Mss., Hist. Mss. Com., 10th Report, App. IV, pp.
254 to 262, etc. One of these documents is a petition by the
Graemes to be sent to some other part of the kingdom (p. 254). In
July, 1587, the 11th parliament of James VI passed an act providing
for the removal of the Graemes to the inland.

[94] C. B. P., II, 323.

[95] Ibid, 547.

CHAPTER VIII

BORDER FINANCE

It is not possible to give more than the approximate cost to the crown of border government. The state papers contain many errors of account and are inextricably confused. The extraordinary expenses, such as were incurred through Elizabeth's interference in Scotch troubles, or the rebellion of the Northern earls, or the preparations made to resist the Armada, should not properly be included in the cost of the defence of the borders. On the other hand the cost of maintaining the garrison and works at Berwick would seem fairly to belong in such a list of expenses. The same may be said of the cost of the extra garrisons which were from time to time levied by the wardens especially to protect the borders from the raids of the Scotch. In the cost of the borders to the crown should also be included the amount of the taxes (subsidies, and fifteenths and tenths), which were regularly remitted by the provisions of the statutes, as well as the reduction in rents which the queen allowed to many of her tenants in consideration of special preparation for defence to be made by them.

The amount allowed by the queen to the Middle and West Marches seems to have varied but little.

In 1560, the charge of the Middle March was £726, 13s. 4d. and of the West March £1,000,[1] but in 1563, after the appointment of Sir John Forster and of Lord Scrope, the charge is given as £1,030 4s. 2d. for the Middle March and £1,046 6s. 7d. for the West March.[2] At the time of Lord

[1] C. S. P., For., 1559-1560, 715.
[2] Burghley Papers, Haynes, I, pp. 397-401.

Scrope's death, June 13, 1592, he was receiving £424 as
the Warden of the West March, and £221 as Captain of
Carlisle. These fees were at that time paid to the warden
without their use being directed, but it was the custom in
earlier years to state how much of the total was to be paid
to the warden serjeants and other officers.[3]

Sir John Forster for his fee as warden received at his
appointment £333 6s. 8d.[4] To this was added £26 13s. 4d.
for the keeping of Tynedale and Redesdale and after 1571,
a further sum of £6 7s. as bailiff and receiver of the forfeited lands of the Earl of Westmorland, who had been
attainted for his part in the Rising of the North.[5] Lord
Hunsdon on his appointment as warden of the Middle
March was granted a total fee of £357 6s. 8d.[6]

The difference between the fees of the wardens and the
charges for the two marches is made up by adding to the
personal fee of the warden of the West March the cost of
the garrison of the Castle, City and Citadel of Carlisle,
and the fees of the Captain of Bewcastle. The fees of the
Keeper of Harbottle Castle, the Land-serjeant of Tynedale and Redesdale, the Master of Ordnance for the North
Parts, the Captain of Tynemouth Castle and the Captain
of Norham Castle, with the allowance for their officers and
servants, and the fee of the Captain of Holy and Farne
Islands were included in the cost of the Middle March.[7]

The fee of the warden of the East March at the beginning of the reign of Elizabeth was 700 marks and of the
Captain of the Castle of Berwick 100 marks. Besides
these, there is a long list of officers, garrisons, and serv-

[3] Sadler State Papers, II, p. 21; C. S. P., Dom., Add., 1580-1625,
Eliz. XXXII, 55; C. B. P., I, 781, 787.
[4] Sadler State Papers, II, p. 21. The fee was 500 marks.
[5] C. B. P., II, 122.
[6] Rymer, Vol. VII, pt. i, p. 6.
[7] Burghley Papers, Haynes, I, pp. 397-401. It is curious that
Norham should be included financially in the Middle March, although it was geographically in the East March.

ants allowed by the "Establishment" which brings the total charges up to £2,776 1s.[8] In 1563, the total fees of the governor and warden were £890 13s. 4d.,[9] but this was probably to permit the Earl of Bedford to pay a deputy warden and a deputy governor. By 1591, Lord Hunsdon's fee as warden had been increased to £424 per year and his fee as Governor of Berwick to £666 13s. 4d., a total of £1,090 13s. 4d.[10]

At the beginning of her reign, Elizabeth had a garrison at Berwick of nearly two thousand men, with total charges, including the fees of the warden and officers and including the cost of fortification and repairs of about £25,000 per year.[11] In 1560, this extraordinary garrison was reduced about one-third, so that the total annual cost of Berwick and the East March was approximately £23,000.[12] In the same year the charges for the works, which included the repair of the fortifications and the up-keep of the bridge over the Tweed was £8,020 for six months to September, and for the last quarter an additional sum of £2,678 10s. 11d.[13] In 1561, it cost nearly £30,000 to pay the garrison and workmen[14] and the cost was about the same in 1562 and 1563.[15] The improved relations with Scotland led to efforts to diminish this expense. As a result of these efforts Sir Valentine Brown made in 1563, a proposition for a new establishment for Berwick by which the total charge for the offi-

8 C. S. P., For., 1563, 409.
9 C. B. P., I, 537.
10 C. B. P., II, 1308; "Charges of the Crown Revenue," pp. 40, 41.
11 Sadler State Papers, II, pp. 7, 8, 11; C. S. P., For., 1558-1559, 601; ibid, 1559-1560, 402, 454, 455, 1228.
12 C. S. P., For., 1560-1561, 541, 542, 543, 604, 690; ibid, 1564-1565, 185.
13 Ibid, 590, 913.
14 Ibid, 1561-1562, 749.
15 Ibid, 1562, 423; ibid, 1563, 873; ibid, 1564-1565, 217, 185.

cers and garrison would be reduced to £14,018 19s. 7d.,[16] and an alternative establishment was suggested by which the cost might be still further reduced to something less than £9,000.[17] The actual total of the charges for the garrison as reduced is given as £12,100 15s. 10d.[18] Thousands of pounds were still being spent on the works, so that the total payments for this year were nearly £20,000.[19] In 1565, owing to increased expenditure on fortifications the charges amounted to over £30,000,—£18,000 for the garrison and £13,000 for the works, and the next year the cost was about the same.[20]

During the period of the Rising in the North, the expenses at Berwick and elsewhere along the border rose enormously for a few months,[21] the total amount increasing to £60,000.

In the year 1575, the charges for the garrison at Berwick were nearly £13,500,[22] and in 1577, the sum had increased to £22,622.[23] Another account shows the expenditure for works for two and one-half years prior to May, 1578, to have been about £5,000.[24] The treasurer of Berwick, who had charge of the disbursements for the garrison and works reported on the 29th of September, 1578, that he had expended £49,751 18s. 8¼d., in three years, giving a total of about £16,500 per year;[25] still another account gives a total payment of a little over £68,000, in four

[16] Ibid, 1563, 409.
[17] Ibid, 1350.
[18] Ibid, 1564-1565, 185.
[19] Ibid, 708.
[20] Ibid, 1566-1568, 592, 627, 628, 629, 739.
[21] C. S. P., Dom., Add., 1566-1579, Eliz. XVII, 8; entries for years 1569-1570, passim; Sadler State Papers, Vol. II, pp. 84-187.
[22] C. S. P., For., 1575-1577, 379.
[23] C. B. P., I, 20; C. S. P., For., 1575-1577, 824.
[24] C. B. P., I, 28.
[25] Ibid, 35.

and one-half years, which averages about the same amount
per year. This sum seems to include from £2,000 to £2,-
500 spent each year on the fortifications, since the regular
charge for the East March and Berwick for 1578 was
£15,000.[26]

In 1581, there is a sudden reduction in the amount
spent for works to £1,148,[27] which reduction is continued
for some years since the total amount spent on repairs
from October, 1582, to May 1, 1583, was only £24 11s.[28]
In 1585, the payments for garrisons and works were £16,-
922 1s. 6d.[29] In 1588, the garrison at Berwick had been
reduced in cost to £12,562 per year[30] but by 1590, the total
had risen again to over £15,000,[31] of which the works cost
£1,117.[32] In 1591, the total charge was again reduced to
£14,353.[33]

By 1593, the payments to the soldiers and officers were
made semi-annually,[34] and for that year the total of two
payments is about £15,000, for 1594, £14,500, for 1595,
£15,000,[35] and for the rest of the reign of Elizabeth the
cost of Berwick and the East March remained at about
the latter figure.

In addition to these sums the Master of the Ordnance
in the North was allowed from the exchequer sums vary-
ing from £900 to £1,300, as is shown by memoranda which
appear from time to time in the state papers.[36]

[26] Ibid, 27; State Papers, Borders, XX, ff. 29-36; "Collection of
Ordinances for the Royal Household," p. 261.
[27] C. B. P., I, 108.
[28] Ibid, 154.
[29] Ibid.
[30] Ibid, 648.
[31] Ibid, 687.
[32] Ibid, 686.
[33] Ibid, 735.
[34] Ibid, 655, 669.
[35] Ibid, 869, 894, 981; C. B. P., II, 190; "Charges of the Crown
Revenue," pp. 40, 41.
[36] C. B. P., I, 19, 85.

A percentage of Elizabeth's pension to the King of
Scotland may, with a certain propriety, also be charged
to the cost of the borders. In February, 1588, for example, Lord Hunsdon wrote to Burghley to request him
not to haggle over £5,000 to the Scotch king since his
friendship is cheap at the price. The soldiers on the
borders had already cost £1,000 and would cost £10,000 by
Michaelmas if she stuck over it.[37] In a succeeding letter
Hunsdon stated that he had asked Carmichael, one of the
Scotch wardens, what were James' wants and the an-
swers suggested were, that James should be made the second person in the realm, and that he should receive £5,000
per year.[38] Just what understanding was finally reached
is not certain, but in the eight years from 1586 to 1593,
James received a total of £27,000, and in 1594, £6,000.
He claimed that he should have received £4,000 per year,
but the queen denied having granted it.[39] Perhaps Robert Bowes' complaints of Elizabeth's parsimony refers to
earlier suggestions of a pension to the King of Scots.[40]

Besides these payments there are from time to time
other payments on account of special levies of troops for
border defence. When these were sent from Berwick the
expense was, of course, included in the charges of that
garrison. Sometimes, however, there was a special warrant under the Privy Seal authorizing the warden to employ, and the receiver of the county, or some other official,
to pay these extra troops. Of such a sort was the permission granted to Sir John Forster in 1585, to maintain a
garrison at Harbottle for three months at a cost of £322,[41]

---

[37] Ibid, 588.
[38] Ibid, 589.
[39] Ibid, 988; Letters of Elizabeth and James, Cam. Soc. Pub., Vol.
79, pp. 29-34.
[40] Correspondence of Robert Bowes, Surtees Soc. Pub., XIV, pp.
252, 260, 283, 296, etc. (1582).
[41] C. B. P., I, 282.

and a similar garrison in the West March in that year which cost the queen from £300 to £400.[42]

The garrison at Berwick was provided with food through a "Victualler" who was under contract to furnish the soldiers with food at a fixed price. For his services he was allowed a fee of twenty shillings a day for fifteen hundred men, and an extra fee if he provided for more than that number.[43] If his supply was short he issued tickets which were supposed to be equal in value to the food, but which were actually taken at a heavy discount by the towns-people. The victualler kept an account with each man and at pay-day was paid by the treasurer the amount of his accounts, which sum was deducted from the pay of the soldiers.[44] While provisions were cheap there was no trouble, but when they became scarce, as they did in the latter part of Elizabeth's reign, the victualler issued more tickets than provisions,[45] especially for the dearer foods, thus almost causing the garrison at Berwick to mutiny.[46] The difficulty was finally solved by allowing the victualler an extra sum from the exchequer which was intended to make up for his loss in supplying goods to the soldiers at less than the market prices. In 1587, this surcharge was about £2,000, and in 1597, it was £2,-316.[47] While these are the only definite records of such payments it seems probable that there were others, especially in the later '90's.

It may be assumed that the cost of the Middle and West Marches did not vary very far from £1,000 each for the whole of the reign of Elizabeth, and that Berwick and the East March cost about £30,000 up to about 1575, giving a

[42] Ibid, 219, 270, 306, 320, 373.
[43] Ibid, 13, 875.
[44] Ibid, 401, 829.
[45] C. S. P., For., 1572-1574, 680; C. B. P., I, 515, 797.
[46] C. B. P., I, 797, 823; C. B. P., II, 9, 12, 24, etc.
[47] C. B. P., I, 797; C. B. P., II, 95, 770.

total charge on the Borders, exclusive of any extraordinary
expenses, of about £32,000. From 1575 to 1584, the total
expense of the officers and garrisons at Berwick and in the
marches seems to have been about £18,000. From 1585 on
this cost was increased by the annual pension to King
James to about £22,000. About £2,000 should be added
to this sum in those years in which a surcharge was allowed for victualling Berwick.

Military expeditions, which cannot properly be charged
to border expenses but which undoubtedly did their share
in reducing English losses through raids were also expen-
sive affairs. The state papers give the charges for the
army in Scotland in 1559-1560 as £131,866.[48] The rebellion of the northern earls cost to suppress over £26,000,
according to the state papers and not quite £21,000 according to the statement of the paymaster, Sir Ralph
Sadler.[49] The preparations in the north for defense
against the armada cost about four thousand pounds.[50]
Military assistance given from time to time to the King
of Scots also cost Elizabeth considerable money.[51] In
1573, she paid nearly £7,500 on this account, and in 1581,
£2,000.[52]

Before 1576, there seems not to have been any assigned
source from which the garrison at Berwick was to be paid.
For example, there was in 1560 a warrant to Roger Alford
to pay twenty thousand pounds to Sir Valentine Brown,
treasurer at Berwick, from the treasure received from Sir

[48] C. S. P., For., 1560-1561, 374. Joseph Stevenson, the editor
of that volume, estimates the cost at £232,398; (preface, p. IX).
This estimate includes the indirect as well as the direct cost.

[49] C. S. P., For., 1569-1571, 1087; Sadler State Papers, II, pp.
161-187; C. S. P., Dom., Add., 1566-1579, Eliz. XV, 133.

[50] C. B. P., I, 590, 591, 592.

[51] C. S. P., For., 1572-1574, 1076.

[52] Correspondence of Robert Bowes, Surtees Soc. Pub., XIV, pp.
165, 166.

Thomas Gresham, Her Majesty's agent in Flanders.[53] In 1563, of the total charge, over £2,000 came from the exchequer and over £12,000 from the receivers of various counties by warrants under the Privy Seal.[54]

By the establishment of 1576, however, it was provided that the money for Berwick was to be provided as follows, —by the Receiver of Her Majesty's lands in Lincolnshire, £3,000; by the Receiver of York, £8,000; and, by the Receiver of Northumberland, Richmond and Durham, £4,000.[55] The share of Yorkshire was paid in two instalments of £3,000 and £5,000 and appears to have been about two-thirds of the total receipts from that county.[56] Any additional sums for works, and extra charges for victualling, were usually allowed out of the exchequer or by warrant under the Privy Seal to the receivers of counties.[57]

The officers of the Middle March appear to have been paid by the Receivers of Northumberland.[58] The treasurer of the West March is stated to have been the Receiver of the county of Cumberland,[59] but there is a petition to Lord Burghley on behalf of Lord Scrope in which he begs that the Captain of Carlisle may be paid at Carlisle by the Deputy Receiver of Cumberland instead of at Barney Castle by the Receiver of the Bishopric.[60] At times the Receiver of York was also called upon to pay troops in the West March.[61]

[53] C. B. P., I, 1.
[54] C. S. P., For., 1563, 873.
[55] State Papers, Borders, XIX, f. 220; C. B. P., I, 537, 687, 735, 798, 981; C. B. P., II, 85, 926, 931, etc.
[56] C. B. P., I, 973; C. B. P., II, 185.
[57] C. B. P., I, 28, 58, 706.
[58] C. S. P., For., 1563, 996.
[59] C. S. P., Dom., Add., 1580-1625, Eliz. XXXII, 55; C. B. P., I, 158, 270.
[60] C. B. P., II, 202.
[61] Ibid, 306.

The sums of money that the towns and counties spent on border defence through taxes raised by themselves has not been determined. The amount that the crown sacrificed in uncollected subsidies, and fifteenths and tenths may be measured by the amounts raised from these sources in the earlier years of James. This has been estimated for the border counties at about £1,000, which should be added to the amount regularly expended by the queen on the borders to get the total cost of administering their government. The total sum varies from about £23,000 to nearly £35,000, exclusive of extraordinary charges, which is from five to eight per cent of the average regular receipts of the crown during the reign of Elizabeth.[62]

It is a fair assumption that, in the eyes of the queen and her council, the safety of her kingdom depended in large degree on the safety and order of Berwick and the northern marches. No other reason would seem to justify the comparative willingness with which Elizabeth reconciled herself to expend so much of her revenue on these bleak and wild northern counties.

[62] "An estimate of the revenue . . . of his Majesty" [James I]. The writer gives the average annual receipts of the crown from Michaelmas, anno 38 Eliz. to Michaelmas, anno 43 Eliz. as £450,759, 11s. 9¼d.—Cott. Ms. Titus, B IV, ff. 285-294.

BIBLIOGRAPHY

SOURCES

State Papers, Borders.

The state papers relating to the history of the borders during the reign of Elizabeth are contained in forty-two volumes entitled State Papers, Borders. The border papers for previous reigns are included in the general collection of state papers, usually under the titles "Foreign" or "Scotland," although the documents themselves may relate entirely to domestic matters. The contents of Vols. I to XIX of those at present bound under the title "Border Papers" were originally distributed chronologically amongst the State Papers, Foreign, up to the year 1577 inclusive, and were calendared under that title. These have since been separated from the collection of State Papers, Foreign, and are now in the same series with the later border papers. The remaining twenty-three volumes of the series are calendared in the two volumes of the Calendar of Border Papers. Volume XLII, the last of the series, is not in its proper chronological order. It contains only a long treatise on the fortification of the borders, which should probably be dated 1587 and is calendared in C. B. P., I, 581.

These papers must form the foundation of any work dealing with Border history during the reign of Elizabeth.

Calendar of Border Papers, Vol. I, from 1560 to 1594; Vol. II, from 1595 to 1603; edited by Joseph Bain, General Register House, Edinburgh, 1894-1896.

These volumes contain abstracts of the papers contained in volumes XX to XLII of the State Papers, Borders, spoken of above. On the whole, the second volume is better calendared than the first, in which are found some inaccuracies. Only 22 of the papers in Vol. I are dated prior to 1578.

Calendar of State Papers, Foreign, 12 vols., from 1558 to 1577.

These volumes contain the calendar of the State Papers, Borders, contained in volumes I to XIX spoken of above. The documents are less fully calendared than in the Calendar of Border Papers. One cannot be sure in using this collection whether a given document will be found amongst State Papers, Borders, or State Papers, Foreign.

Acts of the Privy Council. New Series, from 1542 to 1600; edited by J. R. Dasent, 16 volumes, London, 1890-1908.

In the records of the Privy Council is found constant reference to border matters.

Calendar of State Papers, Domestic, Addenda, for the years 1547
    to 1565, 1566 to 1579, and 1580 to 1625; edited by Mary A.
    E. Green.
    These calendars describe many documents which appear to
    have been taken from the State Papers, Borders, for official
    purposes and to have never been returned to their proper
    places. The volume 1566 to 1579 contains much material for
    the Rising in the North in 1569 to 1570.
Documents and Records Illustrating the History of Scotland and
    the Transactions between the Crowns of Scotland and Eng-
    land; collected and edited by Sir Francis Palgrave, 2 vols.
    Commissioners of the Public Records, London, 1837.
    Contains a wealth of material for the diplomatic relations
    of England and Scotland and the internal affairs of these
    countries as they affected border history.
Calendar of State Papers Relating to Scotland; edited by Markham
    J. Thorpe, Esq., 2 vols. Vol. I, 1509 to 1589, Vol. II, 1590
    to 1603; London, 1858.
    These give useful hints as to where material may be found,
    but the calendars are too brief to be of much greater use.
    Not a great deal of material for border history is to be found
    in these papers.
Register of the Privy Council of Scotland, 1st series, 14 vols.
    Vols. I and II, edited by J. H. Barton; Vols. III, etc., edited
    by David Masson. General Register House, Edinburgh, 1877
    to 1895. Volumes I to VI cover the reign of Elizabeth.
The Hamilton Papers. Letters and Papers Illustrating the Polit-
    ical Relations of England and Scotland in the Sixteenth Cen-
    tury, formerly in possession of the Dukes of Hamilton. Ed-
    ited by Joseph Bain; Vol. I, 1532 to 1543; Vol. II, 1543 to
    1590; General Register House, Edinburgh, 1890, 1892.
    Volume II contains much material for border history. The
    papers are given in full and deal largely with English affairs.
Statutes of the Realm, Eleven Volumes, Record Commission.
Rymer's Foedera (Hague Edition). "Foedera, Conventiones, Lit-
    erae," etc., by Thomas Rymer, 3rd Edition, 10 volumes, includ-
    ing index. The Hague, 1741.
Sadler State Papers. "The State Papers and Letters of Sir Ralph
    Sadler, Knight Banneret." Edited by Arthur Clifford, Esq., 2
    volumes, Edinburgh, 1809.
    Usually quoted as edited by Sir Walter Scott, who added only
    a life of Sadler and a few notes. Volume I extends to May,
    1560;—volume II, from 1560 to circa 1584. There are
    some undated papers in the collection. Important for Ber-
    wick and the borders during the War of the Reformation in
    Scotland and the Rising in the North. Volume II contains

Sadler's accounts as paymaster of the army in 1569-1570. The papers are given in full.

Burghley Papers. "Collection of State Papers relating to affairs in the reign of Queen Elizabeth, transcribed from the original papers and other authentic memorials never before published, left by William Cecil, Lord Burghley, and deposited in the library of Hatfield House." Volume I, 1542 to 1570, edited by Samuel Haynes, London, 1740. Volume II, 1571 to 1596, edited by William Murdin, London, 1759.

This work contains considerable material of value for border history, principally in the form of memoranda. It is usually quoted as Burghley Papers, Haynes (or Murdin). Much of the material is included in the following:

Historical Manuscripts Commission:

9th Report:—Calendar of the Mss. of the Marquis of Salisbury ("Hatfield House Papers"; "Cecil Mss.") Eleven parts, 1888 to 1906, covering the period from 1306 to 1601.

These papers contain a great quantity of material to serve for border history.

10th Report:—Appendix IV. "Muncaster Mss." for the work of the Commission for the Borders under James I.

15th Report:—Appendix IV. "Town Records of Berwick." Fragmentary and not of much importance.

Ellis' Original Letters. "Original Letters Illustrative of English History," etc., by Henry Ellis; Series I, 3 volumes; Series II, 4 volumes; Series III, 4 volumes. London, 1825-1846.

A miscellaneous collection of correspondence without any particular arrangement. Contains considerable material especially useful for the cultural history of England, including some correspondence relating to the borders.

Leges Marchiarum or Border Law. Containing several original Articles and Treaties made and agreed upon by the Commissioners of the Respective Kings of England and Scotland, etc. With a Preface and an Appendix of Charters and Records relating to the said Treaties, by William (Nicholson), Lord Bishop of Carlisle; first edition, London, 1705.

Contains most of the treaties concerning the borders, but only two of those made during the reign of Elizabeth. The Appendix contains the list of watches and other regulations provided for by Lord Wharton in 1555, with a list of names of surveyors for enclosures, etc.

A Collection of Ordinances and Regulations for the Government of the Royal Household Made in Divers Reigns, etc. Society of Antiquaries, London, 1790.

The contents of this volume are sufficiently explained by its title.

BIBLIOGRAPHY 123

The Charges Issuing Forth of the Crown Revenues of England, and the Dominion of Wales, etc., by Captain Lazarus Haward, etc., London, 1660.

Purports to be a complete detailed list of the regular expenditures, civic and military. The list is shown by internal evidence to be of the latter part of the reign of Elizabeth, thought it is undated. Inaccurate in places, but useful.

Surtees Society Publications.

Volume 14, Correspondence of Robert Bowes of Aske, Esq., edited by J. Stevenson, London, 1841.

Contains some material concerning the borders, but is principally connected with negotiations with Scotland.

Volume 44, part i, The Priory of Hexham,—its Chronicles, Endowments and annals, edited by James Raine, Durham, 1864.

Contains material to serve for a history of Hexham and Hexhamshire.

Volume 68, "Household Books of Sir William Howard," edited by James Raine.

From this volume can be gathered a good account of the daily life of a northern noble in the period immediately succeeding Elizabeth. Lord Howard was never Warden as has been erroneously stated.

Volume 93, "Extracts from the Records of The Merchant Adventures of Newcastle-upon-Tyne," edited by F. W. Denby, 2 volumes, Durham, 1895-1899.

This contains the records of "The Merchant Adventures of Newcastle," a body which had been separately organized by permission of the Society of Merchant Adventurers of London.

Camden Society Publications.

Volume 40. A Commentary of the Services and Charges of William, Lord Grey of Wilton, K. G., by his son. Edited by Sir Philip de Malpas Grey Egerton, etc. London, 1847.

This book is an account of Lord Grey's services in Scotland during the War of the Reformation.

Volume 78. Correspondence of James VI of Scotland with Sir Robert Cecil and others. Edited by John Bruce, Esq., London, 1851.

Contains letters relative to international affairs.

Volume 79. Letters of Queen Elizabeth and King James VI of Scotland, etc. Edited by John Bruce, Esq., London, 1849.

Some Municipal Records of the City of Carlisle, etc. Edited for the Cumberland and Westmorland Antiquarian and Archeological Society, by Robert S. Ferguson. Carlisle, 1887.

Publications of the Scottish Text Society.

Vols. 42, 43, Historie and Chronicles of Scotland from the Slaughter of King James the First to the ane thousande fyve hundreith thrie scoir fyftein zeir, by Robert Lindsay of Pitscottie; edited by Ae. J. G. MacKay, 2 vols., Edinburgh, 1899.

This and the next mentioned work contain little material relating to border affairs.

Vols. 5, 14, 19, 34. Historie of Scotland by Jhone Leslie, translated into Scottish from the original Latin in 1596, by James Dalrymple; edited by E. G. Cody, Edinburgh, 1888.

Illustrations of British History, by Edward Lodge, Esq. 3 vols., London, 1838.

This contains chiefly correspondence dating from 1513 to 1618, much of which, however, was written during the reign of Elizabeth. A few documents illustrative of border history are found in this collection.

History of Scotland during the Minority of King James, by Robert Johnston, translated from the Latin by Thomas Middleton, London, 1646.

Contains considerable material concerning the quarrels of the Scotch border nobles, but little about their relations with England. There is, however, a good account of the killing of Sir George Heron in 1575.

Memoirs of Robert Cary, Earl of Monmouth, to which is added Fragmenta Regalia, by Sir Robert Naunton. Introduction by the Earl of Orrery, Edinburgh, 1808.

Robert Cary was deputy warden for Lord Scrope, his brother-in-law, in the West March, and for his father, Lord Hunsdon, in the East March, and was commissioned as Warden of the Middle March in 1598. His memoirs were written when he was quite old, and the dates, and in some cases the details, are inaccurate when measured by contemporary sources. The memoirs give a lively picture of some of the raids of the Scots and counter strokes of the English.

Memoirs of Sir James Melvil, of Hall Hill; edited by George Scott, London, 1683.

Melvil was a trusted councillor of James and took part in many diplomatic affairs. His memoirs sometimes touch upon border affairs, especially in their international aspects.

"Description of England," etc., by John Harrison in Holinshed's Chronicles, Volume I, London, 1807.

History of Elizabeth, etc., by William Camden, etc. 4th ed., London, 1688.

There is considerable material about the borders in this work, especially for the War of the Reformation in Scotland and the Rising in the North.

Annales, or a General Chronicle of England, etc. Begun by John Stow, . . . continued to 1631 by Edmund Howes, London, 1631. Contains an account of the Rising in the North.

BIBLIOGRAPHY 125

Annals of Sir James Balfour.
Diary of James Birrell.
Historie of Great Britain, by John Speed. 3rd edition, London, 1632.

In addition to the above, the Mss. touching border history which are contained in the Cottonian and Harleian collections in the British Museum were also examined. Some of these are of first-rate importance, such as, for example, Cott. Ms., Calig., D. II, ff. 169, et seq., containing a summary of the laws of March, with the articles or paragraph of treaties cited upon which each regulation is based. Most of the material in the Cottonian Mss. is found in the section entitled *Caligula.*

SECONDARY WORKS

In this list works dealing with the general history of the English borders are first given, then county histories, and lastly, local and family history; the latter part of the list contains similar works relating to Scotland.

"The Wardens of the Northern Marches," Creighton Memorial Lecture for 1907, by Thomas Hodgkin, B. A., D. C. L., LL. D., pp. 32, with map; London, 1908.

A brief account of the history of the borders and of some of their customs entertainingly told. The map in this pamphlet is inaccurate as to the boundary between the East and Middle Marches.

"The Border History of England and Scotland," etc., by the Rev. George Ridpath, Berwick, 1848.

This volume is a narrative history of the borders. References for most statements of fact are found in the margin.

"The Condition of the Borders at the Union and the Destruction of the Graham Clan," by John Graham, London, 1907.

An account of the transportation of the Graemes or Grahams from the Debatable Lands to the north of Ireland, with a preceding narrative history of the borders.

"A History of Northumberland" undertaken by the Society of Antiquaries of Newcastle-upon-Tyne, edited by John Hodgson, 7 volumes, Newcastle, 1820-1858.

A more or less satisfactory type of the old-style county history. It runs chiefly to genealogy, though containing here and there good material. In volume VI, there is, for example, a transcription of two surveys of the borders, one made in 1542 and the other in 1550, from Cott. Mss., Titus, F. 13, and Caligula, B. 8.

"A History of Northumberland," by various authors; 8 volumes to 1907; Vol. I, Newcastle-upon-Tyne, 1893, to Vol. VIII. 1907.

The above is a county history by parishes and is not yet

completed. Chiefly of genealogical and antiquarian importance.
"Northumberland and the Borders," by Walter White, London,
1859.

A romantic history of border raids and raiders.
"Life in Northumberland during the Sixteenth Century," by William Weaver Tomlinson, London.

An excellent and interesting account of the daily life of the
Northumberland farmers and gentlemen.
"The Victoria History of the Counties of England"; Volume 110,
issued 1909, but some of the intervening volumes not yet published; edited by H. Arthur Doubleday. "A History of Cumberland," edited by James Wilson, M. A., is to include volumes
1 to 4 of this series. Up to the present, only volumes 1 and
2 of the four have been issued.

Volume I, Westminster, n. d., contains geological and scien-
tific information and a general account of the county to about
the year 1200.

Volume II, London, 1905, contains the ecclesiastical, political
and industrial history of Cumberland. Political history from
Roman times to about 1875 is contained in pages 221 to 231;
by Joseph Wilson and R. A. Allison. A good map of Cumberland indicating the castles and towers at various periods
faces p. 276 in this volume.
"History and Antiquities of the Counties of Westmorland and Cumberland," by Jos. Nicholson and Rich. Burn, 2 vols., London,
1777.

The introduction, volume I, contains some valuable material
reprinted from the State Papers and from Mss. in private
libraries. Volume II contains an appendix of documents, charters, etc., relating to the borders.
"A History of the House of Percy" from the earliest times down
to the present century, by Gerald Brenan, Esq., edited by W.
A. Lindsay, Esq., 2 vols., London, 1902.

Brenan is a partisan of the Percies, religious and otherwise.
An important narrative history of Northumberland. Before
Elizabeth, it was seldom that there was not a Percy warden
of one of the marches or holder of an important office in the
north.
"Annals of the House of Percy, 1030-1887," by Edward Barrington
de Fonblanque; 2 vols., London, 1887.
"The House of Howard," by Gerald Brenan and Edward Phillips
Statham, 2 vols., London, 1907.

In addition to the history of the Howard family, this work
contains an account of the relations of the Howards with border affairs.
"History of the Lives and Reigns of Mary, Queen of Scotland,

and of Her Son and Successor, James," etc., by William San-
derson, London, 1656.
    Some account of the incidents of border history from the
    Scotch point of view is found in this work.
"History of Scotland during the reigns of Queen Mary and King
James VI till his accession to the crown of England," by Wil-
liam Robertson. 2 vols., 1778.
    The appendix contains documents relating to border mat-
    ters.
"History of the Church of Scotland" from the year 203 to the end
of the Reign of James VI, by (Abp.) John Spotswood, Lon-
don, 1655.
"History of Dumfries and Galloway," by Sir Herbert Maxwell.
"History of Liddesdale," etc., by Robert Bruce Armstrong. Part
I, 12th Century to 1530, Edinburgh, 1883.
    This book contains valuable material for the early history
    of the borders. Part I is the only part that has been pub-
    lished.
"Historic Tales of Scotland," by Lawson T. Parker. 2 volumes.
    A collection of romantic stories similar to those of Sir Wal-
    ter Scott.
"The Antiquities of Scotland," by Francis Grose, Esq., 2 vols., Lon-
don, 1797.
    This book consists mainly of pictures of the ruined castles
    and towers on the Scotch border, with a page or so of com-
    ment on each.
"Byways of the Scottish Border," by George Eyre-Todd, Selkirk, n. d.
    An account of a pedestrian tour of Scotch border country
    from Moffat eastward to Berwick. Useful for the topography,
    etc., of Scotch borders.
"Tales of the Border"; "Border Antiquities"; and "Border Min-
strelsy," by Sir Walter Scott; various editions.
    Each work contains besides the romantic stories connected
    with the borders, which the books were intended to preserve,
    an introduction or appendix which is sometimes inaccurate in
    details but in the main leaves one with a clear impression of
    life on the marches.
"Border Raids and Raiders," by Robert Borland.
    The scope of this work is sufficiently indicated by its title.
"Chronicles of Gretna Green," by Peter O. Hutchinson, 2 vols.
London, 1844.
    Volume I contains an interesting narrative account of some
    of the raids and incidents of the West Marches of both Eng-
    land and Scotland. Gretna was one of the usual meeting
    places for days of truce between the West March of England
    and that of Scotland.

128   BIBLIOGRAPHY

"A History of the House of Douglas from the earliest times down
to the legislative union of England and Scotland," by Sir Herbert Maxwell, 2 vols., London, 1902.

Good account of the history of the Scotch border and of
the relations between England and Scotland, especially in connection with the struggles of the king with his Catholic nobility.

"The Border Ellots and the Family of Minto," by G. F. Steward
Elliot, Edinburgh, 1897.

The following secondary works were consulted among others
and in addition to the state papers in preparing the chapter on
the financial aspect of border administration.

"The Royal Treasury of England: or, An Historical Account of
All Taxes—from the Conquest to the Present Year," by John
Stevens, London, 1725.

A brief account of the history of taxation in England.

"The History of our Customs, Subsidies," etc., from William the
Conqueror to the Present Year (1741), by Timothy Cunning-
ham, London, 1741.

Four parts in one volume; first part to the end of Reign of
William III.

"Taxation, Revenue and Power," etc., of the Whole British Em-
pire, by Pablo Pebrer, London, 1833.

"History of the Public Revenue," by Sir John Sinclair, 2 vols., 2nd
edition, London, 1790.

"History of Taxation and Taxes, etc.," by Stephen Dowell, 4 vols.,
London, 1884.

"History of Parliamentary Taxation in England," by Shepard A.
Morgan, N. Y., 1911.

The map accompanying this essay is based upon the description of the marches contained in C. B. P., I, 76; C. S.
P., Dom., Add., Eliz. 1580, Vol. 27, No. 44; S. P., Borders,
XLI, 162; collated with the following maps and plans and
with the Ordnance Survey Maps:—S. P., Borders, XX, 138;
Harl. Ms. No. 3813; Old Royal Ms. 18, D. III, f. 66. The
last mentioned is a large county atlas of England, and is
thought to have been the property of Lord Burghley.

APPENDIX A

A List of the Wardens of the Marches during the Reign of Elizabeth and until the Abolition of the Office of Warden.
(Unless otherwise indicated, the term of service in each case lasted until the appointment of the new warden.)

WARDENS OF THE EAST MARCH

Thomas Percy, Earl of Northumberland ..appointed August, 1557.
Lord Grey, of Wilton ....appointed Jan. 23, 1560.
    Lord Grey died December 25, 1562.
Sir John Selby, Deputy Warden, loc. ten. ..appointed Jan 4, 1563.
Earl of Bedford ....appointed Feb. 27, 1563.
   "   "   " ....recalled . . . 1567.
Lord Hunsdon ....appointed Aug. 23, 1568.
    Lord Hunsdon died July 22, 1596.
Sir Robert Cary, Deputy Warden, loc. ten., appointed . . . 1596.
Lord Willoughby (Peregrine Bertie) ..appointed March 25, 1598.
    Lord Willoughby died June 25, 1601.
Sir John Cary ....appointed *circa* July 7, 1601.
    He acknowledges receipt of his commission at Berwick
    on July 11, 1601.

WARDENS OF THE MIDDLE MARCH

Thomas Percy, Earl of Northumberland ..appointed August, 1557.
Lord Grey, of Wilton ....appointed Dec. 22, 1559.
Sir John Forster ....appointed Nov. 4, 1560.
    Sir John Forster was removed from his Wardenry in
    August, 1587, on account of charges made against him.
    Lord Hunsdon, Warden of the East March, was appointed
    in his place during his trial. Forster was acquitted and
    returned to his Wardenry sometime between February and
    August, 1588, but was finally dismissed in September,
    1595.
Lord Eure ....appointed December, 1595.
    He asked for supersession while under charges, January 22, 1598.
Edward Grey, Deputy Warden, loc. ten. during Eure's trial .. 1597.
Sir Robert Cary ....appointed *circa*, March 25, 1598.
    On this date Lord Willoughby took the East March, of
    which Sir Robert Cary had been Deputy Warden.
George, Earl of Cumberland ....appointed June 8, 1603.

WARDENS OF THE WEST MARCH

William, Lord Dacre ....appointed March 7, 1559.
Henry, Lord Scrope ....appointed April 6, 1563.
    Lord Scrope died June 13, 1592.
Sir Richard Lowther, Deputy Warden, loc. ten., appointed 1592
    Lowther was still Deputy Warden on March 10, 1593.
Thomas, Lord Scrope ....appointed early in 1593.
    (After March tenth and before May first.)
George, Earl of Cumberland ....appointed June 8, 1603.

APPENDIX B

Breviate of attempts on West March by Liddesdale, 1581. (Calendar of Border Papers I, 101.)
"West March Anglie. A Breviat of thattemptates comytted by the Lyddesdaills Scotishemen within thoffice of Bewcastle and other plaices within the West wardenrie of Englande upon thinhabitantes their since Easter last past 1581.—

THE COMPLANANTES.	THOFFENDORS.	THATTEMPTES COMYTTED.
28 Marcij 1581. Jeffraie Sowrebie.	Upon thArmstranges of the Calfhils and Kynmont sonnes with their complices . . . lx Scotischemen.	xij old oxen, x old kye and all thinsight of his howse.
2 Aprilis 1581. Isabell Rowtledge weadowe.	Upon thEllotes . . . 30 men.	iiijor old oxen, vj old kie, one horse and all thinsight of hir howse.
12 Aprilis 1581. James Rowtledg of tHill.	Upon thEllotes and their complices . . . 50 men.	viij old oxen, xij old kye, one meare and all his insight.
iiijo Junij 1581. Richtie Rowtledg.	Upon thEllotes and their complices . . . 80 men.	xxx*tie* old kye, fortie old oxen, taking with open daie forraie.
24 Junij 1581. Malle Nixson and Johane Nixsons, pore wedowes.	Upon thEllotes and their complices . . . 24 men.	xv*ten* old kye, ix old oxen.
26 Junij 1581. John Rowtledg, Jerardes John.	Upon the Crosers and Ellotes.	ix horse and naiges.

THE COMPLANANTES.	THOFFENDORS.	THATTEMPTS COM-YTTED.
Sir Symond Musgrave knight, capten of Bewcastle.	Upon thEllotes and their complices . . . c men and above.	xltie old kye, xxtie old oxen, and the taking of Thomas Rowledg of Todholles Englisheman prisoner, and his horse.
12 Julij 1581. James Forster sonne to Adam.	Upon thEllotes and their complices . . . c men.	xxtie old kie, xvten old oxen, all thinsight of his howse, and the wounding and mamynge of Thomas Batie and Lowrie Forster Englishemen.
14 Julij 1581. Archie Nixson.	Upon thEllotes and their complices . . . c men.	30 old kie and oxen, the spoile of thinsight of his howse and two of his neighbors.
Julij 1581. James Forster of Synywhait.	Upon thEllotes and their complices . . . c men.	50 kie and oxen and all his insight.
Ulto. Julij 1581. Georg Armstrange.	Upon thEllotes and their complices.	xvten kie and oxen, one horse, all his insight, and his sonne wounded verie sore in peril of death.

INDEX

Advowry, 50n.
Alnwick, 9.
Askerton, 10.
Assizes, 17, 18, 19.

Baughling, or bawlching, 72.
Beacons, 96.
Berwick, 7, 8; cost of garrison, 112, 113, 114; disputes with warden, 37; garrison of, 97; goods to be customed at, 55; inhabitants in, 60; taverns in, 60; victualler, 116.
Bewcastle, 9, 10; garrison at, 98; independent of warden, 12.
Blackmail, 58-59.
Bloody shirt, the, 74.
Borders, cost of, 116-119; divisions, 2; inhabitants to be removed, 109; map, 4.
Border law, sources of, 46.
Border militia,—assembly, 93, 94; from Berwick, 98; from Durham, 93; other places, 98-99; sent to Ireland, 101.
Border service, 57n.

Carlisle, 9; garrison, 98; goods customed at, 55; offers border service, 101.
Castles, to be maintained, 91.
Colonies, to be placed in Tynedale, 109.
Commission of wardenry, 25; to be read at warden court, 80.
Commissions for redress, 75-79; authority over wardens, 47, 75, 76, 79; ineffectiveness, 79; procedure of, 77-79; proclamation to be made, 77, 79; settle disputes, 75-76.
Commissions for survey, 102-105; authority 56; Durham to issue, 56; Duchy of Lancaster to issue, 56; ineffectiveness, 57; proposed, 61; reports of, 8, 102, 104, 105.
Coroner, 19-20; of Norham, 11.
Council of the North, 43; lawyer's fees, 43n; relation to warden, 45; reports to Privy Council, 44; meets once a year on the borders, 43.
County Palatine, of Durham, 93; of Hexham, 12.
Courts, oyer and terminer, 17, 80; of assize, 17, 18, 19; quarter sessions, 17; leet, 21; see also Warden court.

Days of truce, appointments not kept, 72; assurance of peace at, 67, 73, 74; baughling or bawlching at, 72; disputed procedure at, 68; disturbed, 72; frequency of, 65; ineffectiveness of, 70-74; meeting places for, 64-65; not to be held by deputy, 48; perjury at, 69; procedure at, 65-70; to be held in uniform manner, 50; to be proclaimed, 66; treaties not followed at, 66.
Debatable lands, 3-7; difficulty of administering justice in, 5-6; efforts to divide, 7; how

133

usurped, 6; offenders escape punishment, 53; value of, in the West March, 5.
Decay of tenantries, 104, 106-108.
de excommunicato capiendo, writ not enforced, 33.
Durham, county of, to provide militia, 93; to issue commissions, 56.

East March, cost of, 111, 112; musters in, 92-93; paymaster, 118; taverns in, 60.
Enclosures, ordered by commissioners, 102; destroyed, 103.
Escheats, 19, 21, 27.

Felony, 85; compounding of, 87-88.
Feuds, 69, 88.
Fifteenths and Tenths, not levied on borders, 59; probable yield, 119.
File, to, a bill, 27; on honor, 69; wrongfully, march treason, 83.
Following the trod, 48, 49, 74.

Gilsland, 13.
Graemes, The, 5, 17, 20, 41; proposals to transport, 108-109; their independence, 13-14; treatment by Elizabeth, 14.
Grahams, *see* Graemes.
Grand jury, 78, 81.

Harbottle, 8, 9.
Hexham, 9, 12; independent of warden, 11.
Holy Island, 11; garrison, 98.
Houses, cost of, 104.

Inhabitants, on borders, 92; Redesdale and Tynedale, 84.

Inheritances, landed, divided, 106.

Jurisdiction, of civil courts, 18, 36.
Justices of the Peace, 18; authority of compared with warden, 38-39; ignorance of, 20; to perform duties, 20; venality of, 21.

Lancaster, Duchy of, 56.
Leet courts, 21.
Liddisdale, independent of Scotch warden, 70-71.

Map of the Borders, 4.
Marches, boundaries, 2-3; 108.
March traitors, 84; tried in warden court, 84-85.
March treason, 60, 81, 82, 84, 85, 88; felony, 85; disputed, 87, 107; penalty, 85-86.
Market court, 20.
Master of Ordnance of the North, 107, 114.
Middle March, cost of, 110, 111; musters in, 92-93; taverns, 60.
Middle Shires, 61.
Militia, sent to borders, 98, 99; paid by county, 100; cost, 115.
Musters, 91-93.

Naworth, 10.
Norham, 8; coroner of, 11; garrison, 98; independent of warden, 11.

Officials, county, in the marches, 16.
Oyer and terminer and gaol delivery, courts of, 17.

Passports, 30, 60.

Petit jury, 81.
Privy Council, chooses wardens,
23; complaints to, 41; inter-
feres in trivial affairs, 42;
relation to warden, 41-43.
Prisoners—right of challenge,
81; kept at York, 70; supported by own nation, 70.

Quarter sessions, courts of, 17.

Red hand, the, 74.
Reprisals by wardens, 31-32.
Rising in the North, cost of,
113; militia for, 99.
Roman Wall, 107.

Sawfee, 51n.
Scotch, intermarry with English, 89, 107, 108; in marches,
89, 90; to be deported, 90.
Sheriff, 18, 19; to assist warden, 19, 85; of Norham, 11.
Shooting of meetings, 72.
Slew dogs, 96, 97.
Star Chamber, 42n.
Statutes relating to the borders, abolition of border law,
61; abolition of warden courts,
62; against blackmail, 59;
commissions for survey, 56,
57; conveyance of supplies to
Scotland, 54; defining authority of wardens, 54; goods to
be customed at Carlisle or
Berwick, 55; horses not to be
exported to Scotland, 55-56;
not enforced, 60, 89, 90;
Scots to be driven out of England, 55; to be proclaimed on
the borders, 55, 56, 59.
Subsidies, not levied, 59; probable yield, 119.

Taverns, in marches, 60.
Treaties with Scotland, 46-47;

provisions of, 47-52; not ob-
served, 52; not voided by
war, 47, 50.
Trod, or troade, hot, 74.

Warden court, abolished, 62;
grand jury, 81; miscarriage
of justice, 87, 88; jurisdiction, 86; petit jury, 81; to
be proclaimed, 80.
Wardens, admiralty authority
of, 34; and recusants, 33-34;
appointing power, 29-30; appointment, 22-24; as justices
of the peace, 33; authority
compared with justices of the
peace, 38-39; commission, 25-
26; convert escheats, 19;
council of, 27; custos rotulorum, 84; fees, 26, 110, 111,
112; hold other offices, 24;
instructions to, 26-28; conflicts with other officials, 35-
39, 79, 88, 107; malfeasance
in office, 39-40; not to deal
with inferior Scotch officials,
73; office not established by
law, 53; policy of Elizabeth
with respect to, 23; power
should be increased, 107; relation of the Council of the
North to, 43-45; relation of
the Privy Council to, 41-43;
reprisals on Scotland by, 31-
32; to reside in march, 28-29;
power to arrest out of march,
35-36; tenure of office, 24, 39;
to account for escheats, 27;
sheriff to aid, 85; to hold musters, 30; to obey Lieutenant
of the North, 26; to seize
malefactors from other parts,
33; violate provisions of treaties, 52.
Wardens, Scotch, lack of authority, 70, 71.

Wark, 8.
Watches, 95; plump watch, 95n.
Water-bailiff, 34; messenger for warden, 35.
West March, cost of, 110, 111;

musters in, 92; paymaster, 118.
Westmorland, part of West March, 2; not depended on, 93.

CPSIA information can be obtained at www.ICGtesting.com
Printed in the USA
LVOW01s1936080414

380849LV00028B/1039/P